The Beauty of Modesty

{ CULTIVATING VIRTUE IN THE
FACE OF A VULGAR CULTURE }

DAVID & DIANE VAUGHAN

CUMBERLAND HOUSE
NASHVILLE, TENNESSEE

THE BEAUTY OF MODESTY
PUBLISHED BY CUMBERLAND HOUSE PUBLISHING
431 Harding Industrial Drive
Nashville, Tennessee 37211

Cover design: Unlikely Suburban Design
Book design: Mary Sanford

Unless otherwise noted, scripture quotations are from THE NEW KING JAMES VERSION. Copyright © 1979, 1980, 1982, Thomas Nelson, Inc., Publishers.

Scripture quotations noted KJV are from the KING JAMES VERSION.

Library of Congress Cataloging-in-Publication Data
Vaughan, David J., 1955–
  The beauty of modesty : cultivating virtue in the face of a vulgar culture / David Vaughan & Diane Vaughan.
    p. cm.
  Includes bibliographical references.
  ISBN 1-58182-422-X (pbk. : alk. paper)
  1. Modesty—Religious aspects—Christianity. 2. Virtue. 3. Christianity and culture. I. Vaughan, Diane, 1963– II. Title.
  BV4647.M63V38 2005
  241'.4—dc22

                                                                2005008189

Printed in the United States of America
1 2 3 4 5 6 7—11 10 09 08 07 06 05

TO JAMES DOBSON AND DONALD WILDMON

Who have done so much to maintain decency in America

CONTENTS

Acknowledgments

This is probably the best part about writing a book. The part where you get to acknowledge all the people in your life who have played a part to help you reach for something you believed God called you to do. They are the many faces of grace sent from the Lord to help lighten the load. Anything done for the Lord and His kingdom always has a price. Left to ourselves, we would surely be overcome by the cost of the steep climb. But because of many, instead of *being* overcome, we *have* overcome.

Just as in the old classic *The Pilgrim's Progress*, these many faces of grace have been to us as *Faithful, Christian's* companion. As they made their way up the steep climb to the *Celestial City, Christian* spoke words to *Faithful* that echo from our hearts to all those we now acknowledge: "*I am glad that we are together and that God has tempered our Spirits, that we can walk as companions in this so pleasant a path.*"

Our path, though at times steep and treacherous, has been bearable because you have been there with us through the years. Yes, we are glad that we are not alone. And since we are not alone, it is only right to acknowledge the part you have played in seeing the pages of this work become a reality.

Our first thanks go to those we hold most dear, our beloved children. Hannah, Lydia, Ethan, and Adam are God's richest blessing in our lives, and to them we owe many thanks for being so patient while we were finishing the manuscript. Without a word of complaint, they waited and prayed for their parents to do the best they could do for Jesus. We were amazed at their gracious spirits to us during this time.

We are also very grateful to God for the spiritual giants in our path whose writings, teaching, and encouragement have helped shape the kind of Christian warriors we have become. To learn as students from them would be enough of a kindness indeed, but to be called their friends over the years, we are at a loss for words. We want to thank you, George and Karen Grant and Doug and Nancy Wilson, for all you have put into our lives.

The staff at Liberty Christian Church are those faithful faces of grace that the Lord placed in our lives to see often, sometimes on a daily basis. Thank you for your endless support and constant presence in our lives. You have encouraged us to stay on the path God has called us to. We desire to thank our wonderful worship director, Marty Kinsey, and his wife, Tami, who lead us week after week to worship the Lord Jesus. We are thankful to our dedicated deacons and their wives, Jim and Sue Hancock, Bryan and Debbie Short, Tom and Mary Ann Otley, and Robert and Jeannie Witty. Thank you for sharing the load of watching over and caring for the flock at Liberty. We also want to thank Mike Bond, our church administrator, and his wife, Andrea. Mike has been such a blessing and recent help in David's calling to pastor, write, and teach.

Our youth director, Timothy Ward, has upheld the standard of modesty for many years among our teens. We are grateful for his leadership and teaching in this area throughout the years we have known him. His devoted wife, Kim, has been an exemplary model of modesty to us and to so many young women who have been touched through their ministry, Teens for Christ. We are very grateful for their support and friendship and have been blessed to co-labor in ministry with them.

The last of Liberty's staff we wish to acknowledge is Pastor Dave Volz and his dear wife, Katherine. They have not only been faithful companions throughout the years, but also faithful servants in whom grace has become quite obvious. Thank you for your willingness to serve in the office of elder over us and to all at Liberty Christian Church. Your humble leadership and love for the Lord have brought us much comfort and joy.

We would also like to thank Donald Eckert, both father and father-in-law, for raising his children in the Christian faith and for modeling moral integrity in the home. His faithfulness to his wife, Joyce (Diane's mother), "in sickness and in health" has left an indelible mark upon our hearts. We have learned of love's commitment in spite of a world run amok with divorces made quick and easy.

Other treasured friends whose support and prayers were coveted during this time were Dave and Cindy Wilson, Jim and Cathy Cummings, Rob and Karen Graham, Wayne and Carolyn Carson, and Denis and Jo Ann Boyle. Thank you for being there and encouraging us in your own special ways. Your companionship over the years has been a blessing to us.

Our publisher, Ron Pitkin, has given us the wonderful opportunity to write our first book together as husband and wife. For this we are very grateful and extend many thanks for his generous kindness and belief in the need for the message of modesty to be written in book form. We are also thankful for the editing work of Mary Sanford. Thank you for your patience as we slowly made finishing touches to the manuscript. It was our desire to be true to the mind of Christ on the virtue of modesty. For this reason, the book took longer to complete than we had originally anticipated. Who would have ever thought so much could be said about modesty? Kendra Hoag, to whom we also owe thanks, prepared some of the research for the book. Thank you, Kendra, for taking the time to get Dr. Vaughan all of the "stats" he was looking for.

All in all, we look to the Lord to reform the morals of His people. And if He can in some small way use this book to that end, we will be contented authors. That modesty has been lost somewhere in this life is quite evident given the sensual environment that saturates our society. But if somehow the beauty of this virtue can be understood in the pages of this book and then written by the Spirit of God upon the heart, then modesty will be found once again. Found to reflect in the bride of Christ to the glory of God. This is our hope and our prayer.

Preface

Modesty matters. It matters to men. It matters to women. It matters to children. And last but not least, it matters to God. Though tossed aside as an ugly old rag of a distant culture, modesty is really a beautiful virtue of the finest fabric that never does go out of style. We have only forgotten how beautiful modesty really is. Or perhaps, we have never had the opportunity to look at modesty for what it is really worth.

As we have spoken to groups across the country about the beauty of modesty, one group stands out. It stands out because of how one young woman responded after hearing the modesty message. When we finished speaking, several teens approached us with their comments and questions. As we listened and made our way through the group, one young woman remained. She began to tell us how the message had affected her. She pointed to her waist and to what, to our surprise, was duct tape, which she had used to connect her short shirt to her hip-hugging jeans. She told us how the Holy Spirit convicted her during the course of our message because she was wearing a shirt baring much of her midriff. Immediately after the meeting, she found some duct tape and taped her shirt to her pants. Condemnation was not the motivation. Nor was she trying to make light of the truth she heard. In all seriousness, she thanked us for helping her know how beautiful modesty truly is. Something clicked with this young woman. And that something was the truth of knowing that modesty matters. Indeed, it mattered to that young woman, who left with eyes to see *The Beauty of Modesty*.

On another occasion, we were approached by a discouraged man who, while trying to worship the Lord during a church service, could not because of an immodestly dressed woman sitting beside him. One would think that in a church of God where the saints assemble for their weekly worship, women would dress appropriately. This, unfortunately, is not always the case. The man said he wanted to ask the woman if she would mind covering her exposed long legs with his coat. The woman's short and tight black leather skirt and high-heeled boots were, to say the least, a huge distraction for him. Because he did not want to "offend" the woman, he kept silent. With his worship interrupted, he sat knowing that modesty did indeed matter to him.

And what about modesty and children? Does it really matter to them? Yes, truth be told, it does. Take, for instance, our own child. One day she received as a gift a CD of a popular Christian music artist, and later showed us how she had colored in the cover insert because the scantily dressed musician needed to clothe herself more modestly. Without any prompting from us, she thought the woman would look prettier with more clothing—so more clothing she added. Now, after her coloring touch-ups, our daughter's eyes liked what she was looking at. We liked our child's touchups too, and really could not believe all the color she had to add. We wondered, however, why our daughter had to do this in the first place. Wasn't this a *Christian* CD? Yes, it was. And that made it matter even more to our daughter.

Surely we can see through these three true-life stories that modesty matters. If it matters to the individuals in the stories, what does that say about God's view of modesty? If a mere woman, man, and innocent child can dimly see something worthy in modesty, what kind of beauty must the thrice-holy God clearly see in it?

It is our desire that *The Beauty of Modesty* will help the Christian community clothe itself with virtue. In the church's commission to be both "salt and light," it is essential to understand that our present time demands God's people to dress like God's people. Yet God's people must not only clothe themselves externally but, more important, they must clothe themselves internally, seeing with the eyes of the heart the beautiful virtue that modesty truly is. Obtaining this kind of godly knowledge, touched by God's grace, helps to clothe the hidden person of the heart. And if the heart is changed, then the body will follow. If the heart is altered, then walking in modesty will be something we will desire to continually nurture throughout our lives. The heart of the matter of modesty will be a revealing reality as we come to understand how much it really does matter—to men, to women, to children, and especially to a holy God.

Why, exactly, does modesty matter? Read on and see.

I

The Need for Modesty

Like Macbeth, Western man made an evil decision, which has become the efficient and final cause of other evil decisions. Have we forgotten our encounter with the witches on the heath? It occurred in the late fourteenth century, and what the witches said to the protagonist of this drama was that man could realize himself more fully if he would only abandon his belief in the existence of transcendentals . . . from this flowed those acts which issue now in modern decadence.

RICHARD WEAVER, *IDEAS HAVE CONSEQUENCES*

Today men expect to be able to treat all women like prostitutes, only without just compensation, and the virgins are the ones who are now stigmatized.

WENDY SHALIT, *A RETURN TO MODESTY*

Few ministers touch upon this subject in their public discourses; and indeed it is not very easy to treat it with propriety from the pulpit. Yet whatever is unsuitable to the Christian profession, an inlet to temptation and productive of evil consequences, should in some way or other be noticed, by those who have the honour of the gospel, and the welfare of their fellow-creatures at heart.

JOHN NEWTON, *THE WORKS OF JOHN NEWTON*

1

The
Right
Approach

If you are blind or from another planet, you may conceivably have missed the fact that modesty has disappeared. It is dead and buried! If you don't think so, go shopping with a teenager.

BARBARA HUGHES

MODESTY HAS FALLEN OUT of fashion. Indeed, it is fair to say that since the sexual revolution of the sixties, modesty has ceased to be a serious subject of discussion. Not only were many of our sexual mores buried beneath the radical rhetoric of "free love," but the very notion of virtue itself became obsolete as we substituted self-expression for self-control and subjective values for objective truth. But what began as a dream of paradise regained ended in the nightmare of the serpent's seduction. We find it difficult to talk about modesty because after a generation of sexual liberation, we have become desensitized to the flesh. While gazing at the exposed female bodies that greet us in every shop, on every television program, in every workplace, we ask with a boorish frown, "Modesty? What's that?"

WHAT MODESTY IS NOT

Since there is such widespread ignorance about modesty, the best place to start is to explain what we are *not* talking about. And the best summary of what modesty is *not* is given by James Spiegel:

- Modesty is *not* bashfulness. The modest person freely chooses to keep certain things private and he does so out of respect for others as well as himself. The shy person's timidity, on the other hand, is not a choice. He keeps things private inadvertently, out of fear. His real concern is not others but himself. Whereas the bashful person finds revealing himself in public uncomfortable, the modest person keeps a thing out of public view for the sake of others, even if he would personally be comfortable revealing more.

- Modesty is *not* shame. To be ashamed of one's physical characteristics is a psychological problem and has nothing to do with modesty. If anything, it militates against the real display of the virtue. Modesty is motivated by self-respect and appreciation for one's own body, and it's because of this bodily self-respect that the modest individual keeps it private.

- Modesty is *not* symptomatic of sexual hang-ups. To be modest is not to oppose sexual expression but the vice of lasciviousness. In a sex-obsessed culture, the healthy balance will necessarily appear unhealthy, as when modest behavior is characterized as a sign of sexual repression. But the sexually repressed person covers up compulsively, not by a choice to respect others and himself. The modest person, in fact, proves

his psychological health in so far as he demonstrates self-control and a keen sense of public
decency.[1]

A PRELIMINARY DEFINITION

So modesty is not bashfulness, shame, or a sexual hang-up.
Then what is it? Noah Webster defines *modesty* as "that
lowly temper which accompanies a moderate estimate of
one's own worth and importance. In females, modesty has
the like character as in males; but the word is used also
as synonymous with chastity, or purity of manners. In this
sense, modesty results from purity of mind, or from the fear
of disgrace and ignominy fortified by education and principle. Unaffected modesty is the sweetest charm of female
excellence, the richest gem in the diadem of their honor."[2]

Wendy Shalit points out, as does Webster, that traditionally modesty embraces two concepts:

> There are two very different kinds of modesty, of
> course. There is, first, modesty in the sense of being
> humble. We say that monks who lead an ascetic
> existence lead a "modest life," or that the person
> who says he doesn't deserve a compliment is being
> "too modest." Then there is sexual modesty, the
> kind we associate with the Medicean Venus or a
> Muslim woman's *chador*. The French have two
> words to keep them straight: *modestie* is the humble
> kind, and *pudeur* the sexual kind. There are also
> two words for the virtue in Latin: *modestia* means a
> respect for decency, restraint (the opposite of *super-*
> *bia*, or haughtiness), and *pudor* refers to a conscious-
> ness of what is decent regarding sexual behavior or
> dress. And the ancient Greeks? Not only did they

9

have *sophrosynes* for self-restraint and *hagneia* to refer to a concern with purity or chastity—that one popped up often on the Stoic lists of virtues or good emotions—but there was also *aischune* for the shame in dishonoring manmade codes and *aidos* for shame or awe in sexual matters.[3]

As we proceed, it will become clear that we disagree that these two kinds of modesty are "very different." In fact, we will argue that they are rooted in the same virtue. But for now, based on the above, we will venture our own working definition of modesty. *Modesty* means "dressing, acting, or speaking with propriety, respect, and moderation." Three words are critical here: *propriety*, which suggests regard for divine or social norms; *respect*, which means regard for others' and one's own conscience; and *moderation*, which is control of one's disposition and habits. Its opposite, *immodesty*, can be defined as: "apparel, action, or speech which is ostentatious, vain, provocative, or sensual; and which thereby reveals a carnal, worldly, or unsanctified heart."

These basic definitions will be "unpacked" as we further consider the nature of modesty. However, please consider a few things about immodesty and modesty, as taught in the Scripture. First, modesty deals with more than apparel or dress. A woman may have her entire body covered and yet act or speak in an immodest way. Note that the apostle Paul in 1 Timothy 2:9 refers not only to apparel, but also to the heart (godliness) and the actions (good works). Throughout Scripture, we see that immodesty may be displayed in more than dress. For instance, look at the "strange" (immoral) woman of the book of

Proverbs. The immoral woman "flatters with her words" (2:16). Her lips "drip honey, and her mouth is smoother than oil" (5:3). She seduces her prey with "the flattering tongue," thus young men are warned: "Do not lust after her beauty in your heart, nor let her allure you with her eyelids" (6:24–25).

Wisdom, the antagonist of the harlot, calls upon young men to keep the law and live.

> Say to wisdom, "You are my sister,"
> And call understanding your nearest kin,
> That they may keep you from the immoral woman,
> From the seductress who flatters with her words.
> For at the window of my house
> I looked through my lattice,
> And saw among the simple,
> I perceived among the youths,
> A young man devoid of understanding,
> Passing along the street near her corner;
> And he took the path to her house
> In the twilight, in the evening,
> In the black and dark night.
> And there a woman met him,
> With the attire of a harlot, and a crafty heart.
> She was loud and rebellious,
> Her feet would not stay at home.
> At times she was outside, at times in the open
>   square,
> Lurking at every corner.
> So she caught him and kissed him;
> With an impudent face she said to him:
> "I have peace offerings with me;
> Today I have paid my vows.
> So I came out to meet you,

Diligently to seek your face,
And I have found you.
I have spread my bed with tapestry,
Colored coverings of Egyptian linen.
I have perfumed my bed
With myrrh, aloes, and cinnamon.
Come, let us take our fill of love until morning;
Let us delight ourselves with love.
For my husband is not at home;
He has gone on a long journey;
He has taken a bag of money with him,
And will come home on the appointed day."
With her enticing speech she caused him to yield,
With her flattering lips she seduced him.
Immediately he went after her, as an ox goes to the
    slaughter,
Or as a fool to the correction of the stocks,
Till an arrow struck his liver.
As a bird hastens to the snare,
He did not know it would cost his life.
Now therefore, listen to me, my children;
Pay attention to the words of my mouth:
Do not let your heart turn aside to her ways,
Do not stray into her paths;
For she has cast down many wounded,
And all who were slain by her were strong men.
Her house is the way to hell,
Descending to the chambers of death.
(Proverbs 7:4–27)

The immoral woman is characterized not only by provocative or seductive attire, she uses words, actions, and facial
expressions to send sensual messages to her hapless victim.
Thus, modesty has to do with more than just clothes. It

governs every aspect of our lives. Therefore, we will need to give thought not only to how we clothe our bodies, but also to how we act and speak via our bodies.

Second, and most important, modesty is a matter of the heart. External modesty or immodesty is a reflection of the inner disposition. This may come as a surprise to some who have given little thought to how they dress. But the question to ask yourself is this: Would someone be able to tell that I am a Christian by how I dress? Of course, the broader questions to be asked are these: What does my wardrobe reveal about my worldview? What is the message of my image? Is Christ Lord of my closet?

The woman who "professes godliness"—that is, "devotion to God," which is the heart attitude—is to act and dress in a manner that corresponds to her profession. The internal and external should (and we would argue, usually do) correspond. The one reflects the other. The visible reveals the invisible. This is an unalterable axiom of the spiritual world. Thus, the alarming thing about immodesty in the church is what it reveals about the spiritual condition of so many Christian women. If you were to judge by apparel alone, you would have to conclude that far too many women who "profess godliness" are, in fact, worldly at heart.

We do not mean to be severe; nor are we encouraging a judgmental attitude. This book is not to be used as a stick to beat your neighbor. Rather, it is to be used as a mirror for self-examination. Nor are we suggesting that there is a simple one-to-one correspondence between dress and heart. Life is usually more complex than that. So, it is possible for someone to dress or act inappropriately while being ignorant of it. This is especially true today, since many people (most notably the young) have never been instructed in any form of manners or etiquette. Despite this ignorance, as Christians we must learn to take responsibility for our appearance and behavior, and for the message it may send to others.

OBJECTIONS AND ERRORS

There are wrong and right ways to approach the subject of modesty. Unfortunately, some of the wrong ways have been tried and found wanting. Yet, because they are wrong, they have caused some to reject the subject altogether. Thus, while laying the biblical framework for our discussion, we will also reply to some common objections.

ᴐLegalism

Perhaps the most common objection to modesty is the charge that it is legalistic. Of course, there is a legalistic form of modesty, but that is not what we are proposing. Nevertheless, some who claim that concern about modest dress is legalistic do not actually understand the biblical notion of legalism. Legalism is not a high view of law, whether human or divine; nor is it the recognition of the need for order, structure, and organization. Every sphere of life has, and must have, rules or standards of some sort. The civil government has laws, the family has rules, and the church has standards. To deny this is not liberation; it is blindness. It is the refusal to acknowledge the limitations that come with the created order. It is the demand to be divine—utterly unlimited. And this demand leads to moral and social anarchy, where every man does what is right in his own eyes.

The claim that we are "not under law but under grace"

is true or false based on what is meant. If it means there are no standards of Christian behavior, then it is wrong. The Bible is full of injunctions and commands regarding how we are to live, how to conduct ourselves so that we please God in all we do. Consider this simple passage alone:

> Finally then, brethren, we urge and exhort in the Lord Jesus that you should abound more and more, just as you received from us how you ought to walk and to please God; for you know what commandments we gave you through the Lord Jesus. For this is the will of God, your sanctification: that you should abstain from sexual immorality; that each of you should know how to possess his own vessel in sanctification and honor, not in passion of lust, like the Gentiles who do not know God; that no one should take advantage of and defraud his brother in this matter, because the Lord is the avenger of all such, as we also forewarned you and testified. For God did not call us to uncleanness, but in holiness. (1 Thessalonians 4:1–7)

Or how about this one:

> I beseech you therefore, brethren, by the mercies of God, that you present your bodies a living sacrifice, holy, acceptable to God, which is your reasonable service. And do not be conformed to this world, but be transformed by the renewing of your mind, that you may prove what is that good and acceptable and perfect will of God. (Romans 12:1–2)

Paul is not a self-help guru dispensing human advice, and these are not just "apostolic opinions" that we can disregard at will. They are, like so many other passages, divine commands: "For you know what *commandments* we gave you . . . this is the *will of God*." Could anything be clearer? Apparently not; for many Evangelicals live in open disregard for the Word of God and yet are warmly welcomed into our churches. Not only do women regularly dress immodestly, but we know that pornography use is rampant as well, not to mention the prevalence of promiscuity, especially among our teens. These are only a few of the many moral lapses plaguing the church. But what they demonstrate is the profound degree to which moral relativism has invaded Evangelicalism. Of course, the church has always had to deal with sin. In fact, it is a society of sinners. Yet the problem today is not just that we sin, but that we don't call it sin. We justify it. We rationalize it. We say, "God has *not* said." Like some in Isaiah's day, we are calling "evil good, and good evil." And we all know what God thinks of that.

The revealed will of God concerning moral behavior is obligatory. Some things are wrong (lust, adultery, etc.), and some things are right (purity, modesty, etc.). We do not have the authority to come up with a manufactured morality by choosing which passages we happen to like—in other words, no smorgasbord Christianity. We are bound to obey the Word of God because it is His Word, and as our Creator and Lord, His Word is authoritative and binding.

When the Bible says that we are "not under law but under grace," it means that the basis or ground of our acceptance with God—our justification—is not obedience to the Mosaic or moral law. The reason for this is not that the law is unimportant but that we fail to keep it. The law is holy, "and the commandment holy and just and good" (Romans 7:12). The problem is that we are fallen and fail to keep the law. Thus, it can only condemn us, never justify us. As Paul said: "We know that the law is spiritual, but I am carnal, sold under sin" (Romans 7:14). We are justified, then, by grace and not by law.

What is legalism then? Perhaps the best definition is given by William Fairweather in his book *The Background of the Gospels*. First of all, legalism magnifies the ceremonial at the expense of the ethical. It emphasizes rituals over morals. Therefore, its primary focus is external rather than internal. The Pharisees, praying in public and doing alms before men, were clearly preoccupied with external appearance. Second, this distortion leads to a confusion between "great moral duties versus little points of casuistry."[4] This is the problem Jesus was addressing when He told the Pharisees to first take the beam (a very large sin) out of their own eye before judging their brother for a splinter (a small offense) in his. And when He rebuked them for tithing mint and cumin (small spices), while forgetting mercy and justice (large virtues).

Third, legalism also assumes a predominantly negative and judgmental character. For instance, Ben Sira, a Jewish rabbi, said: "Give to the good man, help not the sinner." And this negative attitude toward others leads, fourth, to a "narrow particularism," or a spirit of arrogant separation. The end result is a lifestyle of false pretences, or as Fairweather put it: legalism "fostered an atmosphere of unreality; that is, as long as outward appearances were kept up, they [the Pharisees] were content."[5]

Now, many of these legalistic tendencies can be found in the part of Evangelicalism that is reacting to the church's cultural accommodation. While placing a major emphasis on family and childrearing, the tendency of some of these groups is to focus on external compliance while not nurturing internal affections. Thus, children are dressed in Edwardian outfits and trained to "sit still" and "behave" in church, yet their hearts are barren or in some cases outright rebellious. Within the same groups there is the impulse to be negative and exclusive, where righteousness becomes defined as "touch not, taste not"—that is, *don't* watch this, *don't* read that, *don't* go here, *don't* go there. The biblical doctrine of separation is thus perverted to such a degree that the legalistic Christian family can't even find a "pure" church that won't "taint" their innocent children.

And while this is happening—that is, while the legalistic remnant is passing negative judgments on both the world and the church, and while it will not descend from its "holy mount" for fear of being infected by the unclean—all the while it pontificates about raising "warriors for God" and "world-changers for Christ." This is exactly what Fairweather means by "an atmosphere of unreality." It would be comic if it were not tragic: the reality is that far too many Christian children are as carnal as the cat next door. And instead of changing the world, the world is changing them. Legalism doesn't work because it doesn't touch the heart. Or, to be more accurate, it does touch the heart, but not for good. What legalism breeds in the heart is not purity but hypocrisy and rebellion.

Pietism or Subjectivism

Pietism has much in common with legalism, but where it differs is in its overemphasis on the subjective or emotional. The subjectivist denigrates the external as irrelevant, worldly, or unspiritual. All that matters is what happens "in the heart." This produces a radical division between the internal and the external, the spiritual and the secular.

As a result, we get certain odd phenomena like the Christian who just gushes with warm, fuzzy love (*love* being one of his favorite words), but who won't lift a finger to save the helpless babies who are ruthlessly slaughtered every day. "Abortion?" the pietist puzzles. "Why, that's political! And we all know that politics is worldly." "What? Preach against abortion?" protests the pietist pastor. "But that might offend someone's sensibilities, and that would be unloving."

A perfect personal example of the pietistic disconnect between heart and hand was seen in a worship service we once attended. In the praise service the pastor exhorted the church members to raise their hands as an act of devotion during one of the songs. Many of the members did so. But after the service one of the members commented to us, "I didn't raise my hands when he told us to because I was already raising my hands in my heart." Ironically, the Scriptures specifically command men "to lift up holy hands" (see 1 Timothy 2:8), yet for this pietist it was enough to do so "in my heart." Thus the internal trumped the external even to the point of disregarding a command of Scripture. But if a biblical command requires an act rather than a disposition, then the only way to fulfill it is by performing the external act.

Closer to our issue of modesty, we get the strange phenomenon of a young woman who goes to church while dressed like Madonna (and we don't mean the mother of Jesus). "Me?" she says in horror when confronted about her appearance. "Cause a brother to sin?

Incite young men to lust? That was the farthest thing from my mind."

Perhaps; but what goes on in the mind or heart is not the standard we live by. The Bible is. And here is where legalism and pietism are in secret league: both substitute the human for the divine. The legalist substitutes human traditions; the pietist substitutes human feelings. If the pietist has all the "right feelings," then she has done her duty. There is a chasm, however, between feelings and action. It is a form of spirituality that is misapplied by not being applied at all. It lives in the netherworld of mind and emotions and does not descend to the mundane tasks of everyday living.

ᏬChristian Relativism

A Christian, by definition, believes in absolutes. So the relativist we have in mind here is not necessarily someone who outright denies the existence of absolutes. On the contrary; the Christian relativist insists that if we don't have "chapter and verse" on a subject, then we must be silent. In the name of orthodoxy we are being told that if a certain practice cannot be backed up by chapter and verse, then it is illegitimate. Of course, this kind of thing sounds very spiritual. We must beware, however. For once you get on the chapter-verse omnibus, you will find yourself on the "Fundamentalist Freeway," which leads to "Pharisee City," a whitewashed cemetery filled with dead men's bones.

Fundamentalism notwithstanding, not everything the Bible addresses is spelled out in detail. Nor need it be. The Bible tells a husband to love his wife, for example, but it doesn't say to buy her flowers. There is no "chapter and verse" for that particular expression of love. Yet that expression is, nevertheless, a legitimate application of the command.

Since the biblical teaching on modesty is not very detailed, the cultural relativist will say: "Since the Bible doesn't give us a dress code, there is no standard at all." The error here is confusion over "application vs. principle." It is true that the Bible does not give us a detailed dress code with exact specifications ("A hemline must be so many inches long, etc."). But what it does give us is principles that we can and must apply to our own cultural situation. Learning specifics is important. And where the Bible gives us specifics, we should learn them—and obey them. However, learning specifics requires only knowledge, whereas learning and applying principles requires wisdom and maturity, which is why a dress-code approach is so appealing to the fundamentalist.

Moreover, the error of cultural relativism also shows confusion about "ends and means." One reason the Bible does not give us a "specific dress code" is because that is not the "end" or "goal" of modesty. The purpose of modesty is to beautify the body and to protect from lust and immorality, not to make us look as if we stepped off an assembly line. The purpose of modesty is to divert time and attention away from a mere physical beauty and to point it to a moral and spiritual beauty. A dress code cannot do this. As we study the subject of modesty, we will see that there are a number of important biblical principles to master and enact.

Parochialism

A final wrong approach to modesty is what we call parochialism. This is the attempt to freeze fashions in a particular historical era. For instance, it is not uncommon to see Christian product catalogs with a host of Victorian images. The impression is that femininity and modesty can be reduced to certain (past) historical fashions like long dresses, hair buns, lace head-coverings, and other fashions germane to that era. This fashion may be an example of modesty, but it is not the standard of modesty. Of course, if a woman likes that fashion, she is surely free to dress that way. But what is not permissible is for her to then impose on others her taste in fashion.

The answer to parochialism is simple: if modesty can be achieved by an exact replication of a historical fashion, then why not go back to the first century and dress like Jesus? The fact is, no historical era per se is the standard of modesty. We do not have to dress in outdated fashions to be modest. It is possible for a Christian woman to be attractively dressed in a contemporary outfit while still retaining her modesty. And like the other errors mentioned, parochialism wants to rest in external appearance. Real biblical modesty, on the other hand, deals with both the heart and the appearance. To deal only with externals does not go to the root of the problem.

2

Worldview and Ward- robe

Relativism is the most banal of evils, masquerading as a disinter- ested party. Relativism destroys the soul of culture by whispering in a thousand ways that justice is a fantasy, that morality is entirely subjective and therefore situational. But morality is not artificial. It is as natural as air and as necessary for survival as the human institutions it sus- tains.

ROBERT H. KNIGHT

THE PROBLEM OF IMMODESTY IN the church is really a symptom of other problems, one of which is the moral condition of our society. The leading social indicators show that America is a culture in decline. We have failing marriages; adultery; teenage suicide and promiscuity; homosexuality and lesbianism; pornography and obscenity in print, music, and movies; transgenderism; self-mutilation; urban gangs; suburban violence and drugs; and the list could go on.

Why is this happening? Why are our teens killing themselves at an alarming rate? Why do we have "Goth" cults and the likes of Marilyn Manson? Why are we subjected to perverse and violent rap music or grotesque and brutal pornography?

In one sense, the answer is actually fairly simple: ideas have consequences. We must understand that what we believe, that is, our worldview, really does make a difference in how we live. And when a culture—our culture—adopts the ideology of secularism and moral relativism, then perverse results will naturally follow. Let us explain.

Historians agree that the survival of any society depends upon some unifying system of thought. This system, or "cultural glue," is what we call a worldview. It is a way of looking at things, says R. C. Sproul, which "conditions how we interpret the meaning of daily life."[1] A worldview is made up of a group of presuppositions or ideas. And as Richard Weaver has pointed out, "Ideas have consequences." Thus, ideas are not neutral. They can and do have either positive or negative consequences.[2] How we live reflects our deepest-held convictions.

For centuries, the "Enlightenment Project" has been at war with the Christian worldview. Perhaps best termed "secularism," this worldview emphasizes the worldly or temporal over the spiritual or eternal. It focuses on the "here and now"—this world—and neglects the spiritual and eternal world.

The secular world believes that God is dead (or irrelevant to everyday life) and that man is the measure of all things. There is no absolute authority, no universal truth, no fixed standards of behavior. Man is the ultimate norm. Having dethroned God, man is now his own god reigning in his own universe. Since morals are relative, the final test of behavior becomes personal preference. Thus, secularism is profoundly hedonistic, where everything becomes relative to "my wishes." Pleasure becomes the measure.

The irony of secularism is that it claims to exalt man's place in the universe: by eliminating God, man becomes a god. However, Western civilization's high view of the dignity of man was based upon the biblical doctrines of creation and redemption. And the humanist's attempt to retain human dignity without its biblical foundation has dismally failed. As Os Guinness wrote:

> The humanists claimed that they could retain Christian values and give them validity independent of God. But Nietzsche dismissed this as impossible since Christianity was the entire undergirding of all Western civilization; not only of its religious beliefs but also of its social values and its fundamental view of man. He [Nietzsche] diagnosed, not progress, but a time of decadence whose logic is nihilism. There remains only the void. Man is falling. His dignity is lost. His values are gone.[3]

This loss of human dignity is also related to the humanist's belief in the theory of evolution. Man is no longer a special creation of God made in His image, but merely a product of random chance, a child of nature. Sociologist Arthur Custance has noted: "Man passed from his superior position as unique creation to the lesser position of being only the link in a chain, a link which was not essentially of any greater importance than any other link."[4] According to the evolutionary scheme, the primordial importance of the individual is completely subverted. Individuals are simply a means, not an end, of evolution. As a result, the actual individuals count for nothing.[5]

Along with the loss of dignity, there is a profound loss of meaning in secular modernity. Shakespeare's lines from *Macbeth* could serve well as our secular creed:

> Life's but a walking shadow, a poor player
> That struts and frets his hour upon the stage,

And then is heard no more; it is a tale
Told by an idiot, full of sound and fury,
Signifying nothing.[6]

Modern secularists concur. For example, Sartre, in his novel *Nausea*, puts these words into the mouth of his leading character: "Every existent is born without reason, prolongs itself out of weakness and dies by chance."[7] Albert Camus is just as bleak: "I proclaim that I believe in nothing and that everything is absurd."[8] Perhaps more than any other spokesman for secular humanism, Bertrand Russell penned modernity's most mournful eulogy:

> That man is the product of causes which had no pre-vision of the end they were achieving; that his origin, his growth, his hopes and fears, his loves and beliefs, are but the outcome of accidental collocations of atoms; that no fire, no heroism, no intensity of thought and feeling, can preserve an individual life beyond the grave; that all the labours of the ages, all the devotion, all the inspirations, all the noonday brightness of human genius, are destined to extinction in the vast death of the solar system; and that the whole temple of man's achievement must inevitably be buried beneath the debris of a universe in ruins—all these things, if not quite beyond dispute, are yet so nearly certain, that no philosophy which rejects them can hope to stand.[9]

"What," you might ask, "does all this have to do with modesty?" Listen to Yeats's poem "The Second Coming":

Turning and turning in the widening gyre
The falcon cannot hear the falconer;
Things fall apart; the center cannot hold;

Mere anarchy is loosed upon the world,
The blood-dimmed tide is loosed, and everywhere
The ceremony of innocence is drowned;
The best lack all conviction, while the worst
Are full of passionate intensity.[10]

Moral anarchy is loosed upon our society, and the result is that "innocence is drowned." Virtue is under attack as decadence, unchecked, tramples on civility. As Gertrude Himmelfarb put it, "The beasts of modernism have mutated into the beasts of postmodernism—relativism into nihilism, amorality into immorality, irrationality into insanity, sexual deviancy into polymorphous perversity."[11] This "polymorphous perversity" is a nice phrase for the utter sexualization of our culture. Everything from automobiles to fast food is now sold using erotic images of women. Wherever we look—magazines, books, advertisements, billboards, movies, and television—we are harassed by the sensual and seductive female icon. In effect, "every phase of our culture has been invaded by sex. Our civilization has become so pre-occupied with sex that it now oozes from all pores of American life."[12] And where sensuality thrives, modesty withers.

James Spiegel, in his book *How to Be Good in a World Gone Bad*, points out the impact of our culture on modesty:

These factors—the mainstreaming of sexual
deviancy and the widespread belief in the moral
autonomy of human beings [relativism]—combine
to create a cultural atmosphere in which the virtue
of modesty is a relic. Where deviancy is normalized,
modesty cannot be seen as having any practical
value. Where moral absolutes are rejected, the con-

cept of shame, upon which the concept of modesty crucially depends, is unintelligible. Today the moral tables have completely turned. The modest are frequently lampooned as prudish, hung-up, or old-fashioned. It's not uncommon for the trait to be represented as a character flaw or as symptomatic of a psychological problem. Among the virtues, none is so portrayed as a vice in our culture more often than modesty.[13]

Perhaps the most telling sign of the loss of modesty is the pervasiveness of pornography, the most daring act of immodesty. Commenting on America's moral revolution, Maggie Gallagher commented, "Sex was remade in the image of Hugh Hefner; Eros demoted from a god to a buffoon. Over the last thirty years, America transformed itself into a pornographic culture."[14] Indeed, we have. According to Hebditch and Anning, in 1988 annual worldwide sales revenues of sexually explicit material were in excess of $5 billion, much of this in video sales. And although a 1989 *Wall Street Journal* article claimed that porn was on the decline, Eric Schlosser, of *U.S. News and World Report*, reported that in 1996 the United States spent $8 billion on pornography, which is more money than Hollywood's total domestic box-office receipts. The sex industry worldwide was bringing in $20 billion.[15]

According to the publication *Adult Video News*:

- Hard-core video rentals rose from $75 million in 1985 to $665 million in 1996.
- 150 new hard-core video titles are created each week.
- Adult pay-per-view movies garnered $150 million.

- Phone sex business is estimated at $750 million
  to $1 billion a year.[16]

Now that secularism has reduced men and women to the status of mere animals, we find them behaving accordingly. As a result, we have the grossest forms of pornography, where sex is treated as an animalistic appetite and where people debase themselves by treating each other as objects for personal consumption. Since people are being told that they are nothing more than brute beasts randomly produced by evolution, it is not surprising that they are now acting according to script. Pornography logically flows from the secular tenet that man is a mere animal, because pornography appeals to a man's animal appetite for sex. Where there are no moral absolutes, pleasure seeking becomes an unrestrained and uninhibited lifestyle. And if sex is no longer sacred, no longer God's precious gift to those who keep covenant in marriage, but a mere biological urge, then why not indulge it to the fullest? Living in a meaningless world, why not find "authenticity" in the existential orgasm?

When we see an immodest woman, what are we seeing? Not only a lot more flesh, but a lot more *than* flesh. We are seeing the incarnation of a worldview—but it is not a Christian worldview. It is a pagan one. In his book *No Place for Truth*, David Wells notes "six important points about the pagan mind, each of which has at least its echoes in the modern mind":

1. Insofar as they were known, the gods were known through nature. Pagans began with the experiences of nature and from this generated countless myths about the activities of the gods

that explained why life had turned out the way
it had or why it had yielded the experiences
that it had.

2. Pagans proceeded from the basis of their experience to understand the supernatural. Apart
from nature there was no other revelation,
and apart from experience there was no other
means of knowing the intent of the gods. The
pagan mind did not search for truth so much as
it looked for the meaning of experience.

3. The supernatural realm was neither stable nor
predictable. The gods inflicted calamity on the
earth either because of the surfacing of some
dark intent within themselves or because of the
outbreak of rivalries and territorial disputes. It
was the uncertainty over these intentions that
produced the system of appeasement represented by the pagan religious rites.

4. The pagan divinities were sexual, and this
meant that their religion had sexual overtones
as well. Cult prostitution and an intense inter-
est in fertility and reproduction (evident in
child sacrifice and other rites) were common.
Sexual rites were accorded considerable celestial significance and were viewed as a means of
identifying with nature's rhythms and placating
the gods when disharmony broke out.

5. It is obvious that the pagan mind had no moral
categories superseding the relativities of daily
life. Pagans made no appeal to moral absolutes.
They determined what was right experimen-
tally. . . . Pagan religion sought to bring society
into harmony not with moral absolutes but
with the rhythms of life.

6. History had no real value for the pagans; their lives were centered in the experience of the moment. They sought in a variety of ways to cut their ties to the past and to focus instead on the future. They sought out predictable cycles of regeneration in emulation of the rhythms of nature, that annual passage through the seasons from autumnal death to springtime rebirth. And they found history especially irrelevant in their efforts to know the gods; here, too, experience was everything for the activity of the gods in the past offered not reliable indications of how they might act in the future.[17]

Notice that in Wells's description of paganism there is a strong emphasis on two things: experience and sex. These are paganism's hallmarks. Indeed, Christian thinkers have always noted that speculative infidelity, meaning skepticism, leads to self-indulgence and immorality. When a society rejects the truth of God's holiness and His judgment of sin, it slides into sensuality. As William Shedd pointed out more than a century ago:

There are degrees, however, in infidelity; but its influence is the same in kind. It is sensualizing, be it moderate or be it extreme. A man may not deny all the doctrines of the Bible, or all the attributes of God. He may select some and reject the remainder. There is much skepticism of this sort. But the individual will in every instance be guided in his choice by his epicurean inclination rather than by his moral conscience. Is it probable that he will select the strict doctrines and attributes, and reject the others? Will he affirm that God is a consuming

33

fire, but deny that God is love? Will he accept the
doctrine of endless punishment, but reject that of
the resurrection of the body? No; his unbelief will
retain those truths that present little opposition to a
life of pleasure in this world, and will cast out those
that stand directly in the way of it.[18]

Legalized pornography is simply the most blatant
example of our society's acceptance of a pagan worldview.
Indeed, we have sanctioned it and given it our highest
form of endorsement: legalized protection. Yet it is not
the only example of our decadence. Our assault on innocence and modesty now begins quite early in our public
schools. Sex-ed, as it is called, is another legalized means
by which we wage war on virtue with the sanction of our
government. In classrooms all across our nation, children are being subjected to mental rape: their innocence
is being stolen from them against their wills. Schools in
the Northeast teach "Condom Line-Up," where young
boys and girls have to properly arrange pieces of cardboard
with words on them like "sexual arousal," "erection," and
"leave room at the tip." In New Jersey, children in kinder-
garten are taught about birth control and masturbation.
A popular text now in use across the country is titled, *It's
Perfectly Normal,* published by Planned Parenthood. "It
features illustrations of nude, playful boys and girls as they
masturbate on beds and heterosexual and homosexual
couples as they have intercourse in different positions."[19]
Recommended reading age? Ten years old and up.

Another Planned Parenthood publication on sexuality gives this enlightened advice to our teens: "Relax
about loving. Sex is fun and joyful, and courting is fun and

joyful, and it comes in all types and styles, all of which are okay. Do what gives pleasure, and enjoy what gives pleasure, and ask for what gives pleasure. Don't rob yourself of joy by focusing on old-fashioned ideas about what's normal or nice. Just communicate and enjoy!"[20] With "instruction" like this, is it any wonder that our children are brutish and profane and are now being referred to as the "barbarians" in our midst? Why, we have not only lost the virtue of modesty, but we cannot even remember why it should be cherished!

Of course, many more examples could be given: the obscenity of much popular music; the vulgarity of talk shows; the banality of women's magazines. But *for the sake of modesty*, we will spare you. The point to be seen, however, is that the predominant ethos in America—call it secularism, humanism, or postmodernism—this ethos is basically pagan in its outlook. And paganism's rejection of God and His moral law inevitably leads to the degradation of culture and the perversion of sexuality. It always has, and it always will. This is the lesson that Paul urged upon the church at Rome nearly two thousand years ago:

> For the wrath of God is revealed from heaven against all ungodliness and unrighteousness of men, who suppress the truth in unrighteousness, because what may be known of God is manifest in them, for God has shown it to them. For since the creation of the world His invisible attributes are clearly seen, being understood by the things that are made, even His eternal power and Godhead, so that they are without excuse, because, although they knew God, they did not glorify Him as God, nor were thankful, but became futile in their thoughts, and their foolish hearts were

darkened. Professing to be wise, they became fools, and changed the glory of the incorruptible God into an image made like corruptible man—and birds and four-footed animals and creeping things. Therefore God also gave them up to uncleanness, in the lusts of their hearts, to dishonor their bodies among themselves, who exchanged the truth of God for the lie, and worshiped and served the creature rather than the Creator, who is blessed forever. Amen. For this reason God gave them up to vile passions. For even their women exchanged the natural use for what is against nature. Likewise also the men, leaving the natural use of the woman, burned in their lust for one another, men with men committing what is shameful, and receiving in themselves the penalty of their error which was due. And even as they did not like to retain God in their knowledge, God gave them over to a debased mind, to do those things which are not fitting. (Romans 1:18–28)

Here is a worldview that distorts God and corrupts man by exalting pleasure. It is the worldview of ancient paganism, where sensual pleasure and perversion are the goal of life. And it is this worldview that has gained ascendancy in America. Unfortunately, we are now seeing this same worldview ooze into the church.

3
The Cultural Captivity of the Church

Religious consumers want to have a spirituality for the same reason that they want to drive a stylish and expensive auto. Costly obedience is as foreign to them in matters spiritual as self-denial is in matters material.

DAVID WELLS

IF IMMODESTY IS THE INCARNATION of a pagan world-view, then why are we seeing so much immodesty among Christians? Why do we now see women attending church wearing skintight jeans, see-through blouses, or skimpy skirts? Why are Christian women wearing clothes that only a generation ago would have been considered immoral, if not illegal?

The answer is that we are experiencing the cultural captivity of the church. An alien and ungodly philosophy dominates all centers of cultural influence—the media, the academy, the courts; and, sadly, it is beginning to dominate even many churches. As John Whitehead noted more than a decade ago:

> As a thinking being, the modern Christian has suc-cumbed to secularization. He accepts religion—its morality, its worship, its spiritual culture. However,

he rejects the total view of life which sees all earthly
issues within the context of the eternal; that relates
all human problems—social, political, cultural—to
the doctrinal foundations of the Christian faith. As
a consequence, the faith ineffectively fails even to
minimally raise the ethical standards of the American population.[1]

Well-known theologian R. C. Sproul would agree. "I
doubt if there has been a period in all of the Christian history," he said, "when so many Christians are so ineffectual
in shaping the culture in which they live as is true right
now in the United States."[2] To put the matter bluntly: the
salt in America is losing its savor.

First of all, the church is becoming intellectually lazy.
In the eighteenth and nineteenth centuries, religious
thought and institutions in America were dominated by
an austere, learned, and intellectual form of discourse that
is largely absent from religious life today. Whereas once
you would have gone to church expecting a long, doctrinal exposition of a biblical text or doctrine, now we have
"Express Church," where everyone shares their feelings
and insights without any pastoral accountability or doctrinal direction. We used to attend church to worship
God and hear His Word; now we go to feel better and be
uplifted. The focus used to be on God; now it is on self.
David Wells, reporting on a study of sermons published
in modern Evangelical periodicals, noted that "less than
half are explicitly biblical, and a significant number are
not discernibly Christian at all. They could have been
given by a secular psychologist in a setting like the Rotary
Club."[3]

Also, the church has become morally flabby. Pollster George Gallup has said that the United States is facing a "moral and ethical crisis of the first dimension." He said it is shocking to discover that "church attendance makes little difference in people's ethical views and behavior with respect to lying, cheating, pilfering and not reporting theft."[4] And we would add: church attendance often makes little difference in sexual behavior and modesty.

In fact, the case may possibly be worse than Gallup first reported, as the following Barna research suggests. In 1997, 75 percent of Christians said that they found it annoying or bothersome to hear profanity on the radio; 49 percent of Christians did not favor making sexually explicit or pornographic movies and magazines illegal; 19 percent of Christians said that viewing pornographic videos was a matter of taste, not morality; and only 50 percent of Christians said that truth was unchanging and absolute.[5]

Reporting in October 2002, Barna found that whereas "born-again" individuals were twice as likely to not watch a movie because of its rating (27 percent vs. 14 percent), there was no significant difference evident when it came to the likelihood of viewing adult-only content on the Internet, discussing a specific moral issue, or reading magazines or watching videos with explicit sexual content. While he did find that Christian faith made a difference in some moral behaviors, faith seemed to make little impact on other areas. "Some of the elements that are easy to overlook in this study relate to the actual numbers of Christians who do or don't do something that their faith requires of them," Barna commented. "For instance, all Christians are called to regularly pray for their leaders, or to influence other people in accordance with biblical values, but relatively few believers do so. Similarly, while Christians are exhorted to not engage in behaviors such as gambling or filling their minds with inappropriate sexual images through pornography, *millions do so on a regular basis*."[6] "Did he say *millions?*" you might ask. Yes, he did. And we must let the gravity of that fact sink in if we are trying to understand what is happening to the church in America.

A year later, Barna found that of ten moral behaviors he evaluated, three were deemed "morally acceptable" by a majority of Americans: gambling (63 percent); cohabitation (60 percent), which is a euphemism for fornication; and sexual fantasies (59 percent). Another 42 percent said it was acceptable to commit adultery, while 38 percent gave their stamp of approval to pornography. What makes these figures even more shocking is, first, that 84 percent of Americans claim to be Christians, and second, that since these are behaviors that a Christian would normally conceal, the actual percentages may be higher than reported.[7]

It should be noted here just how deeply the sexual revolution of the 1960s has infected the church. All of the activities just mentioned—adultery, fornication (cohabitation), pornography, lust—are of a sexual nature, and all of these are clearly *forbidden* in the Bible. For instance, adultery, which is sexual activity by a married person outside the covenant of marriage, is forbidden in the seventh commandment: "You shall not commit adultery" (Exodus 20:14). So grievous is this sin in the eyes of God that in the Old Testament He actually made it a capital crime: "If a man is found lying with a woman married to a husband, then both of them shall die—the man that lay with the woman, and the woman" (Deuteronomy 22:22) Other Scriptures are to the same point.

Fornication differs from adultery in that it is illicit sex between unmarried persons. And although the Bible recognizes that it is a lesser offense than adultery, it is still a serious violation of Christian morality. The Old Testament required a man to marry the woman that he "humbled," provided the father approved of the marriage. While in the New Testament we learn that the Christian's body is a temple of the Holy Spirit, and to commit fornication is a defilement of God's temple. As the apostle Paul put it: "Foods for the stomach and the stomach for foods, but God will destroy both it and them. Now the body is not for sexual immorality but for the Lord, and the Lord for the body. . . . Flee sexual immorality. Every sin that a man does is outside the body, but he who commits sexual immorality sins against his own body" (1 Corinthians 6:13, 18).

Yet what makes the sexual ethic of the Bible unique is that it goes to the source of our actions, the very thoughts and intents of the heart. It is here, at the heart, that Jesus lays the ax to the root. In His sublime Sermon on the Mount, Christ says that the spirit of the seventh commandment requires sexual purity in our innermost thoughts. "You have heard that it was said to those of old, 'You shall not commit adultery.' But I say to you that whoever looks at a woman to lust for her has already committed adultery with her in his heart." Indeed, so grave is this sin of lust that Christ warns His followers: "If your right eye causes you to sin, pluck it out and cast it from you; for it is more profitable for you that one of your members perish, than for your whole body to be cast into hell. And if your right hand causes you to sin, cut it off and cast it from you; for it is more profitable for you that one of your members perish, than for your whole body to be cast into hell" (Matthew 5:27–30).

So, even though the Bible advocates sexual purity even in one's heart, which is the fountain of all action, we now have an evangelical church where significant numbers not only practice sexual sins, but actually have the hubris to justify it. This is telling evidence of the cultural captivity of the church.

That Christians commit sin is no surprise. That Christians commit *grievous* sin is no surprise. That Christians commit grievous *sexual* sin is no surprise. But what is a surprise—what makes our current situation so alarming—is not isolated sinful behaviors; it is the justification for such actions by way of adopting an alien worldview. To put the matter differently: what we are witnessing is a sweeping secularization of the church in her very mind and morals. Whereas Scripture exhorts us to "not be conformed to the world, but to be transformed by the renewing of our mind," millions of Evangelicals have been acculturated to the point where they are condoning vices that are condemned in the Bible. To fail to live up to the Bible's ethical standards is one thing. As James said, "In many things we all stumble" (James 3:1). But to transform the biblical standard into its opposite is a much more grave offense. Or, should we say, it reveals a far graver problem. As Jesus said: "If therefore the light that is in you is darkness, how great is that darkness!" (Matthew 6:23).

Jesus Christ calls His church the "salt of the earth" and the "light of the world":

You are the salt of the earth; but if the salt loses
its flavor, how shall it be seasoned? It is then good
for nothing but to be thrown out and trampled
underfoot by men. You are the light of the world. A
city that is set on a hill cannot be hidden. Nor do
they light a lamp and put it under a basket, but on
a lampstand, and it gives light to all who are in the
house. Let your light so shine before men, that they
may see your good works and glorify your Father in
heaven" (Matthew 5:13–16).

What does this mean? At a minimum it means that
the church should not be like the world, nor be assimi-
lated into the world, but somehow be different. More fully
it means that the church should have a redemptive impact
on the world. In fact, the purpose of salt is to halt corruption. Thus the church should impact the culture in such
a way that the moral corruption that naturally flows from
fallen human nature is hindered. The function of light, of
course, is to dispel darkness. And in the Bible, "darkness"
is always associated with sin, error, ignorance, and evil. As
the "light of the world," therefore, the church should be
exposing darkness, dispelling ignorance, and conquering
sin.

In a word, the church should be a unique people
whose lives are radically different from the world, being
transformed by the Word and Spirit of God into the moral
image of Jesus Christ. This moral transformation, which
begins with the new birth and continues through progressive sanctification, is first and foremost a transformation
of the mind and heart. It does not end there, however; it
begins there. It ends by touching every area of the Christian's life. In other words, sanctification works its way

out to touch such mundane areas as how we spend our money, what we read or view, and even the decisions we make regarding clothing. Modesty matters because it is an expression of our worldview and a measure of our sanctification. It is an expression of the grace of God operating in our lives and transforming us into the image of Christ.

Now, this does not mean we should all dress alike or dress in outdated fashions. But it does mean that, as we renew our minds, we should think through our lifestyle choices—in every area—informed by the Word of God. And that is the goal of understanding the nature of modesty, to which we will now turn.

II

The Nature of Modesty

*Among the innumerable benefits which the world has derived from
the Christian religion, a superior refinement in the sexual sentiments,
a more equal and respectful treatment of women, greater dignity and
permanence conferred on the institution of marriage, are not the least
considerable; in consequence of which the purest affections, and the
most sacred duties, are grafted on the stock of the strongest instincts.*

ROBERT HALL, *THE NATURE OF MODESTY*

*The real choice in the debate over standards of dress is not between
legalism and license, but between God as lawgiver or man as lawgiver.*

DOUG PHILLIPS IN *CHRISTIAN MODESTY AND THE
PUBLIC UNDRESSING OF AMERICA*

*By dressing in a provocative way, girls and women are actually sexu-
ally harassing men. . . .*

MARGARET BUCHANAN, *PARENTING WITH PURPOSE*

4

A Biblical View of the Body

The problem is that in the end a flesh-and-blood woman cannot compete with the fantasy of the feminine ideal. We always fall short with the messiness of our own bodies.

LILIAN CALLES BARGER

IN OUR STUDY OF MODESTY we must avoid two extremes. One is to focus exclusively on appearance while neglecting the heart. The other extreme is to say that motivation is paramount, thus, it really doesn't matter how we dress. The first extreme favors the legalist; the second favors the Gnostic. Yet in studying modesty we learn that both the inner motivation and the outer appearance are important to God. In order to avoid this ever-swinging pendulum and hold a truly biblical view of modesty, we must understand what the Scripture teaches about the physical body. For only then will we learn to use and adorn our bodies in such a way that pleases not ourselves but our Creator.

The most basic fact regarding the human body is that it was created by God. The original creation account in Genesis states: "The LORD God formed man of the dust of the ground, and breathed into his nostrils the breath of life; and man became a living being" (2:7). It is clear that the formation of man, Adam, here spoken of, relates to both his body and his soul. His body was formed from the dust of the ground, and his soul was breathed into him by God. Thus both body and soul were originally created by God and were good.

Eve's creation differs from Adam's in that she was taken out of man; but notice that Eve was taken from man's body, not his soul.

> The LORD God said, "It is not good that man should be alone; I will make him a helper comparable to him." Out of the ground the LORD God formed every beast of the field and every bird of the air, and brought them to Adam to see what he would call them. And whatever Adam called each living crea-ture, that was its name. So Adam gave names to all cattle, to the birds of the air, and to every beast of the field. But for Adam there was not found a helper comparable to him. And the LORD God caused a deep sleep to fall on Adam, and he slept; and He took one of his ribs, and closed up the flesh in its place. Then the rib which the LORD God had taken from man He made into a woman, and He brought her to the man. And Adam said:
> "This is now bone of my bones
> And flesh of my flesh;
> She shall be called Woman,
> Because she was taken out of Man."
> Therefore a man shall leave his father and mother and be joined to his wife, and they shall become one flesh. And they were both naked, the man and his wife, and were not ashamed. (Genesis 2:18–25)

Two things are noteworthy in these passages: first, the creation narratives of both Adam and Eve mention the formation of their bodies from some preexisting matter. Their bodies were not made of some spiritual substance different from ours. And second, it is explicitly mentioned that their bodies were naked, yet they were not ashamed.

Not only were their bodies made by God, their bodies were originally created good. There was nothing wrong with their having earthly bodies. In fact, like everything else God created, this was "good." Even though they were naked, they did not feel shame, because their bodies were not evil. As we shall see, modesty does not demand the body be covered because it is somehow evil. It isn't. It is Gnosticism, not Christianity, which teaches that the body is inherently evil or the seat of sin. As D. M. Pratt has rightly said,

> It is apparent that the body in itself is not necessarily evil, a doctrine which is taught in Greek philosophy, but nowhere in the Old Testament and New Testament. The rigid and harsh dualism met with in Plato is absent from Paul's writings, and is utterly foreign to the whole of Scripture. Here we are distinctly taught, on the one hand, that the body is subordinated to the soul, but on the other, with equal clearness, that the human body has a dignity, originally conferred upon it by the Creator, who shaped it out of earth, and glorified it by the incarnation of Christ, the sinless One, though born of a woman.[1]

The body is a good creation of God; thus it is to be adorned according to His standards.

But more importantly, the creation of the human body was inseparable from the creation of the human person. In other words, God did not create a disembodied soul, which for a time floated around in the air and then later was trapped in a body. Rather, body and soul were created together. This means that when we think of the human "person," we cannot think exclusively of the "heart," as if the body is some sort of appendage not integral to the person himself. To be human means we have both a body and a soul (some prefer the word *spirit*). Or better, a human person is the *union* of both body and soul.

While it may seem as if we are belaboring the obvious, we must realize how deeply Gnostic thinking has crept into the church. It is not uncommon to hear Christians say that what really matters is "the heart." As with other clichés, this may or may not be true. If it means that God measures our actions by our intentions, then it is true. And if it means that the heart is the source of our actions, then it is true. But if it means that God doesn't really care about what we do with our bodies, then it is radically false. The Bible knows no such dichotomy between the inner and outer person. In fact, as Lilian Barger has pointed out, our bodies help us reflect the divine image:

> Each body-self [i.e., person] participates in the
> divine image, showing humanity's uniqueness
> among other creatures in its spiritual, emotional,
> and intellectual aspects. Though the Creator has
> no body, the divine intent is that the human body
> be an active agent in communicating the image of
> God. Our bodies mediate personality, emotions, and
> creativity; all communicate attributes of God. Our
> bodies make us present even as God is present in a

particular place of belonging. Every single human being reminds us of God's presence through the presence of his or her body. Our face-to-face way of relating makes us personal in all our dealings. Thus to have a body is to make ourselves known.[2]

Moreover, the body, though originally created good, was made subject to the curse of the Fall. The impact of original sin on mankind was that the entire person, both soul and body, was now fallen. The soul became corrupt and prone to evil, while the body became mortal and subject to toil and death.

> Then the LORD God called to Adam and said to him, "Where are you?" So he said, "I heard Your voice in the garden, and I was afraid because I was naked; and I hid myself." And He said, "Who told you that you were naked? Have you eaten from the tree of which I commanded you that you should not eat?" Then the man said, "The woman whom You gave to be with me, she gave me of the tree, and I ate." And the LORD God said to the woman, "What is this you have done?" The woman said, "The serpent deceived me, and I ate." So the LORD God said to the serpent:
> "Because you have done this,
> You are cursed more than all cattle,
> And more than every beast of the field;
> On your belly you shall go,
> And you shall eat dust
> All the days of your life.
> And I will put enmity
> Between you and the woman,
> And between your seed and her Seed;
> He shall bruise your head,

And you shall bruise His heel."

To the woman He said:

> "I will greatly multiply your sorrow and your
> conception;
> In pain you shall bring forth children;
> Your desire shall be for your husband,
> And he shall rule over you."

Then to Adam He said, "Because you have heeded
the voice of your wife, and have eaten from the tree
of which I commanded you, saying, 'You shall not
eat of it':

> "Cursed is the ground for your sake;
> In toil you shall eat of it
> All the days of your life.
> Both thorns and thistles it shall bring forth
> for you,
> And you shall eat the herb of the field.
> In the sweat of your face you shall eat bread
> Till you return to the ground,
> For out of it you were taken;
> For dust you are,
> And to dust you shall return."
> (Genesis 3:9–19)

The body did not, however, become the seat of sin. It
is the soul of man that is the real culprit. The body merely
obeys the soul's sinful commands. Of course, the body may
have disordered desires, and through abuse develop a craving or addiction to certain sins. The initial thrust to sin
comes from the soul's evil response to the physical consciousness. When the Bible speaks of "the flesh," it uses
that term to mean several things, depending on the context. It may mean "mankind." It may mean the "physical
body." But usually it means the "principle of sin" or "old

nature" that still resides in the regenerate saint. It is "the flesh," not the body, that causes us to sin.

> Has then what is good become death to me? Certainly not! But sin, that it might appear sin, was producing death in me through what is good, so that sin through the commandment might become exceedingly sinful. For we know that the law is spiritual, but I am carnal, sold under sin. For what I am doing, I do not understand. For what I will to do, that I do not practice; but what I hate, that I do. If, then, I do what I will not to do, I agree with the law that it is good. But now, it is no longer I who do it, but sin that dwells in me. For I know that in me (that is, in my flesh) nothing good dwells; for to will is present with me, but how to perform what is good I do not find. For the good that I will to do, I do not do; but the evil I will not to do, that I practice. Now if I do what I will not to do, it is no longer I who do it, but sin that dwells in me. I find then a law, that evil is present with me, the one who wills to do good. For I delight in the law of God according to the inward man. But I see another law in my members, warring against the law of my mind, and bringing me into captivity to the law of sin which is in my members. O wretched man that I am! Who will deliver me from this body of death? I thank God—through Jesus Christ our Lord! So then, with the mind I myself serve the law of God, but with the flesh the law of sin. (Romans 7:13–25)

Nevertheless, the body is now fallen and mortal. It is subject to fatigue, illness, aging, and death. It is also now subject to covering. The immediate result of the Fall was a sense of shame that demanded the body be covered. It was not the body, but the soul's evil desires that demanded the body to be covered. After Adam and Eve were fallen, they were no longer safe with each other. Sin set them at odds with one another and with God. It was sin that required clothing as a protection.

Fortunately, the Fall is not the end of God's story. For Christ was sent to redeem us from our sin and free us from all of its evil effects. The salvation accomplished by Christ on the cross was a redemption of the entire person, both soul and body. Jesus did not just die for our souls; He died for *us*, which means He died to save the *entire person*, both material and immaterial. So important is the body in the scheme of redemption that we are specifically told our bodies have been purchased by Christ for residence of the Holy Spirit:

> Foods for the stomach and the stomach for foods, but God will destroy both it and them. Now the body is not for sexual immorality but for the Lord, and the Lord for the body. And God both raised up the Lord and will also raise us up by His power. Do you not know that your bodies are members of Christ? Shall I then take the members of Christ and make them members of a harlot? Certainly not! Or do you not know that he who is joined to a harlot is one body with her? For "the two," He says, "shall become one flesh." But he who is joined to the Lord is one spirit with Him. Flee sexual immorality. Every sin that a man does is outside the body, but he who commits sexual immorality sins against his own body. Or do you not know that your body is the temple of the Holy Spirit who is in you, whom you

have from God, and you are not your own? For you were bought at a price; therefore glorify God in your body and in your spirit, which are God's. (1 Corinthians 6:13–20)

How could we regard our bodies as trivial or unspiritual when the very Spirit of God resides in our bodies as a temple? How can we say, "All that really matters is the heart" when our bodies have been purchased by the precious blood of Christ and are now inhabited by God Himself in the person of the Spirit? So valuable is this earthly temple of the Spirit that "if anyone defiles the temple of God, God will destroy him. For the temple of God is holy, which temple you are" (1 Corinthians 3:17).

Last, we have a promise that our bodies will one day be resurrected and glorified. This is the hope of our adoption and the reward of our physical sufferings.

> I consider that the sufferings of this present time are not worthy to be compared with the glory which shall be revealed in us. For the earnest expectation of the creation eagerly waits for the revealing of the sons of God. For the creation was subjected to futility, not willingly, but because of Him who subjected it in hope; because the creation itself also will be delivered from the bondage of corruption into the glorious liberty of the children of God. For we know that the whole creation groans and labors with birth pangs together until now. Not only that, but we also who have the firstfruits of the Spirit, even we ourselves groan within ourselves, eagerly waiting for the adoption, the redemption of our body. For we were saved in this hope, but hope that is seen is not hope; for why does one still hope for what he sees?

But if we hope for what we do not see, we eagerly
wait for it with perseverance. (Romans 8:18–25)

These basic biblical truths regarding the body provide
many lessons, but we will mention only a few that relate
to modesty.

One lesson is that nowhere in the account of the Creation are we given an ideal of physical beauty. Though
Western artists have sometimes portrayed Eve as a stun-
ning beauty, she is not portrayed that way in Scripture.
She and her body were good; as good as Adam's; as good
as the earth; as good as all of God's creation. If ever there
were an opportunity for God to state "His ideal" of feminine beauty, it would have been here in the creation
account, before the world was marred by sin. But there is
no "ideal" stated. This does not mean, however, that the
Bible is indifferent to physical beauty. In many places
feminine beauty is recognized. Abraham's wife, Sarah, was
"a woman of beautiful countenance" (Genesis 12:11)—so
beautiful, in fact, that the Egyptians thought "she was very
beautiful" (Genesis 12:14). Isaac's wife, Rebekah, was also
"beautiful to behold" because she "was beautiful of form
and appearance" (Genesis 29:17). Other examples could
be given, but the point to note is that while the Scripture
freely acknowledges physical beauty, there is no biblical
ideal.

Notions of physical beauty will vary according to
culture and time. And since there is no divine standard,
women do not have to feel pressured to live up to our culture's manufactured standard of what is beautiful to feel
accepted and loved by God. Our bodies are a gift from
God and do not need to conform to a cultural ideal that

distorts the very purpose of the body. Without question, today's beauty myth is unrealistic. It is the work of very clever advertising designed to exploit a woman's insecurity about her looks. As Barger notes:

> Continual exposure to the media ideal skews reality for all of us. Its effect on the average young woman is a body dissatisfaction rate higher than 60 percent in high school and 80 percent in college. The obsession with weight starts early, with 42 percent of girls in first to third grades expressing a desire to be thinner. According to published research, 15 percent of women would sacrifice more than five years of their life to obtain the weight they desire. There are at least eight million sufferers of life-threatening anorexia nervosa (reported in girls as young as eight years old), bulimia, and other associated eating disorders in America; 90 percent of these are women.[3]

The quest for ideal beauty even drives many women under the knife. Barger again:

> Since 1992, elective cosmetic procedures have risen a dramatic 198 percent. Extreme forms of liposuction, mostly requested by women, can require over ten hours of extensive remodeling of the body. Between 1990 and 1999, the number of facelifts in the United States increased sixfold. And as the horror stories of silicon implants in the 1980s faded from our memories, the 1990s brought a sixfold increase in the number of breast augmentations. In 1999 alone there was a 26 percent increase of the procedure (more than 187,000 surgeries) at the cost of $3,000–$8,000.[4]

A woman's value does not reside in her physical beauty. Her body is God's gift. As an act of creaturehood, she must learn to be thankful for her body, even though it may not meet the cultural "ideal." Moreover, although we have no biblical standard or ideal for what constitutes physical beauty, we do have a standard of what constitutes moral or inner beauty. That standard is nothing less than the very moral character of our Creator Himself, as reflected in the face of Jesus Christ. This is the standard that transcends all cultural expectations. While our body is useful in displaying the *imago Dei* and in fulfilling the cultural mandate, moral beauty, or what we call virtue, resides in the soul. This is the beauty that every woman should strive to acquire. God's essential nature is holy; thus, moral beauty is the soul's acquisition of holiness. Modesty serves to accentuate moral beauty over physical beauty by averting our gaze away from the body.

The second lesson is that the body, being essential to one's personhood, is not a matter of indifference. We must not say that God cares only about the heart. We must not treat our bodies as appendages with no vital connection to our spiritual lives or to our worldview. What we do with our bodies, and yes, even how we clothe them, reflects our worldview, our spirituality, and our virtue. Of course, a carnal person may dress in a modest manner. External modesty may be used as a mere facade. But a spiritual person will not dress immodestly. A person who is dressing or acting in a wanton or ostentatious fashion is someone with an inner problem, either emotional, moral, or spiritual. And that inner problem is manifesting itself in the appearance.

And this leads to the next point, which is that Christ

is the Redeemer and Lord of our bodies. We do not have the authority to abuse our bodies, mutilate our bodies, or prostitute our bodies. Our bodies are not our own. We have been bought with a price, and therefore we must obey Christ with our bodies. We cannot hide behind the Gnostic claim that "in my heart I am obeying God." Oh, really? Then it should be evident in your body—in your actions, looks, words, and dress. For the soul and the body are united. As Sherman has said:

> [The soul and the body] are from God; both should be for God. Man consists of body and soul; the service of man is the service of both. The body is to be sanctified as well as the soul; and, therefore, to be offered to God as well as the soul. Both are to be glorified, both are to glorify. As our Saviour's divinity was manifested in his body, so should our spirituality be in ours. To give God the service of the body and not the soul, is hypocrisy; to give God the service of the spirit and not the body, is sacrilege; to give him neither, atheism.[5]

So, if Christ is Lord of our bodies, then we must seek guidance from His Word on how we are to please Him in the use of our bodies. Our bodies are not autonomous from His Word. Christ rules over all.

5
Modesty and the Law of Christ

*The benevolence and wisdom
of the Author of Christianity
are eminently conspicuous in
the laws he has enacted on this
branch of morals; for, while he
authorizes marriage, he restrains
the vagrancy and caprice of the
passions, by forbidding polygamy
and divorce; and, well knowing that offences and the laws
of chastity usually spring from
an ill-regulated imagination, he
inculcates purity of heart.*

ROBERT HALL

N O CHRISTIAN WOULD DISPUTE THE claim that Jesus
Christ is Lord of all, since the Scripture is replete
with references to His universal lordship. For instance,
shortly before His ascension, Christ prefaced His Great
Commission to His followers with the great claim regarding His lordship: "All authority has been given to Me in
heaven and on earth" (Matthew 28:18). The substance of
the very first Christian sermon in the book of Acts was a
declaration of Christ's lordship:

> Men of Israel, hear these words: Jesus of Nazareth,
> a Man attested by God to you by miracles, wonders,
> and signs which God did through Him in your
> midst, as you yourselves also know—Him, being
> delivered by the determined purpose and foreknowl-
> edge of God, you have taken by lawless hands, have
> crucified, and put to death; whom God raised up,

having loosed the pains of death, because it was not possible that He should be held by it. For David says concerning Him:

"I foresaw the LORD always before my face,
For He is at my right hand, that I may not be
    shaken.
Therefore my heart rejoiced, and my tongue
    was glad;
Moreover my flesh also will rest in hope.
Because You will not leave my soul in Hades,
Nor will You allow Your Holy One to see
    corruption.
You have made known to me the ways of life;
You will make me full of joy in Your
    presence."

Men and brethren, let me speak freely to you of the patriarch David, that he is both dead and buried, and his tomb is with us to this day. Therefore, being a prophet, and knowing that God had sworn with an oath to him that of the fruit of his body, according to the flesh, He would raise up the Christ to sit on his throne, he, foreseeing this, spoke concerning the resurrection of the Christ, that His soul was not left in Hades, nor did His flesh see corruption. This Jesus God has raised up, of which we are all witnesses. Therefore being exalted to the right hand of God, and having received from the Father the promise of the Holy Spirit, He poured out this which you now see and hear. For David did not ascend into the heavens, but he says himself:

"The LORD said to my Lord,
'Sit at My right hand,
Till I make Your enemies Your footstool.'"

Therefore let all the house of Israel know assuredly

that God has made this Jesus, whom you crucified,
both Lord and Christ. (Acts 2:22–36)

It is this lordship of Christ that is the foundation of an
explicitly Christian worldview. Since He is now reigning
over all—that is, all worlds, all nations, and all peoples—
all are called upon to repent and embrace Him as Savior
and Lord. And once they bow the knee to Him, and begin
to grow in knowledge and grace, they then learn that they
must take "every thought into captivity to the obedience
of Christ" (2 Corinthians 10:5). They must understand
every area of life through the lens of Christ's Word and
authority, because every area of life is under His dominion. He is not Lord just of the soul and not the body; or
Lord of the family but not the church or state. Christ's
reign is universal.

As A. A. Hodge has eloquently said:

> The allegiance we owe is not to a doctrine, but to
> a Person, the God-man, our mediatorial King. We
> are bound to obey the Bible in all our actions and
> relations as citizens as well as church-members,
> because it is the law he has promulgated as the rule
> of our action, and because he is our supreme Lord
> and Master. The foundation of his authority is not
> our election, but the fact that he is absolutely per-
> fect and worthy of absolute trust and obedience,
> and that he has created us, continues to uphold us
> in being, supplies us with all that makes existence
> desirable, and that he redeemed us from the wrath
> of God by his blood. His authority therefore does
> not depend upon our faith or our profession. It
> binds the atheist and the debauchee as much as the
> believer or the saint. No man can plead immunity

because he is an unbeliever. Nor can we who are
believers be excused from the consistent ordering
of our whole lives according to his revealed will
because the majority of our fellow-citizens disagree
with us. Let others do as they will; as for us and for
our houses, we will serve the Lord.[1]

As we strive to order our lives according to His will,
we can learn valuable lessons about modesty in Christ's
sublime Sermon on the Mount.

CHRIST AND THE LAW

After telling His disciples that He did not come to destroy
the law but to fulfill it, Jesus then made the remarkable
statement that *their* righteousness had to exceed that of
the Pharisees. What did He mean? Was He telling us that
we must do more and more "good works"—that we must
fast more, pray more, and give more? Thankfully, no.

As we read through the Sermon on the Mount, we see
that the Lord is doing two things. First, He is not correcting the law, as if something were wrong with it. Rather,
He corrects the erroneous interpretations of the law made
by the Scribes and Pharisees, who "made the commandment of God of no effect by [their] traditions" (Matthew
15:6). Neither does Jesus contradict the law; rather, He
is providing clarification of its original meaning or giving
applications to specific circumstances.

And second, He is "spiritualizing" the law; that is, He
is showing us how the law applies not only to our actions
but also to the condition of our hearts. For example, the
law forbids murder, which is an act. Yet the Lord says the
law also forbids anger, an emotion. The law forbids adul-

tery, an act; yet according to Jesus, the law also forbids lust, a desire of the heart. Thus Christ is teaching us to "internalize" the law, and not to rest in mere outward conformity. Though we may comply with the law regarding externals, we must go to the root and observe the law in our hearts.

THE CHRISTIAN AND THE LAW

Christ is teaching us that we, His disciples, must not disregard the demands of the law; rather, as His followers we should not only reverence the law, but we should also understand that the claims of the law extend to even the thoughts and intents of our hearts.

For the believer who has been saved by grace, the law is no longer a terror. It has served its function in bringing us to Christ for salvation. Thus, being under grace, we are not under the law as a means of acceptance with God. We are not justified by the law. However, the law does continue to reveal to us the perfect righteousness of God, and still serves to guide us on the path of holiness. It is a revelation of God's will for believer and unbeliever alike. It has a ministry of conviction and a ministry of instruction. The Christian, being under grace, has the ability to comprehend the spiritual import of the law, and is given both the desire and power to obey the law. God works in him "to will and to do for His good pleasure" (Philippians 2:13).

This obedience, however, is motivated not by slavish fear but by grateful love. It is *evangelical* obedience, that is, obedience born of our response to God's grace revealed in the gospel. We love God because He first loved us. And we strive to obey God and His law as a demonstration of our love. This obedience is internal as well as external.

We obey *in* the heart and *from* the heart. But we obey also *in* the body and *through* the body. We yield our bodily members to God as instruments of righteousness (Romans 6:13). We present our bodies to God as a living sacrifice (Romans 12:1). We "cleanse ourselves from all filthiness of the flesh and spirit, perfecting holiness in the fear of God" (2 Corinthians 7:1).

THE MEANING OF MARRIAGE

In the fifth chapter of Matthew, Jesus continues to expound the true meaning of the law, particularly the spiritual import of the seventh commandment, which is, "You shall not commit adultery" (Exodus 20:14). The Jewish teachers of the day understood adultery in the exclusively physical sense of extramarital sexual relationships. However, the Pharisees nullified the force of the commandment by applying it to the act only, and by allowing easy and unlawful divorces. This, in effect, legalized adulterous relationships.

Christ, on the other hand, expounds the seventh commandment by first internalizing it. Not only is the act of adultery forbidden, but the lustful desire is equally condemned. The act violates the letter of the law, but the desire violates the spirit of the law.

> You have heard that it was said to those of old,
> "You shall not commit adultery." But I say to you
> that whoever looks at a woman to lust for her has
> already committed adultery with her in his heart.
> (Matthew 5:27–28)

Christ also extends the commandment. By locating adultery in the lustful heart, He extends its meaning to "all unlawful [i.e., unbiblical] lust." Thus the varied laws against

polygamy, fornication (premarital sex), rape (or molesta-
tion), seduction, incest, bestiality, and homosexuality may
all be comprehended under the seventh commandment.
All of these acts, and the lusts that incite them, are incom-
patible with God's design and purpose for sexuality and
marriage. The well-known commentator Thomas Scott,
writing on the seventh commandment, says,

> Under the word *lasciviousness*, various transgressions
> are denoted, which cannot be mentioned without
> offence; and everything, which does not comport
> with the spirit of marriage, though sanctioned by
> that name, violates the spiritual meaning of the
> prohibition. All impure conversation, imaginations,
> or desires, are likewise condemned by this law. "He
> that looks on a woman to lust after her, has commit-
> ted adultery with her already in his heart." Writing,
> reading, publishing, vending, or circulating obscene
> books; exposing to view indecent pictures or statues,
> or whatever else may excite men's passions, must
> partake of the same guilt: and wit, elegance, and
> ingenuity only increase the mischief, wherever the
> specious poison is administered. All the arts of dress,
> motion, or demeanour, which form temptation to
> heedless youth; with all those blandishments, insin-
> uations, amorous looks and words, which subserve
> seduction, fall under the same censure. In short, the
> commandment requires the utmost purity, both of
> body and soul, in secret as well as before men; with
> a holy indifference to animal indulgences, and the
> strictest government of all the appetites, senses, and
> passions; and it enjoins the desire and endeavour of
> preserving the same disposition and behaviour in all
> others, as far as we have it in our power.[2]

According to the uniform teaching of Scripture, including the teaching of Christ Himself, marriage is a divine institution founded upon human nature as created by God, in which one man and one woman covenant before God to live together as husband and wife until separated by death. In Matthew chapter 19 Jesus teaches on the nature of marriage:

> The Pharisees also came to Him, testing Him, and saying to Him, "Is it lawful for a man to divorce his wife for just any reason?" And He answered and said to them, "Have you not read that He who made them at the beginning 'made them male and female,' and said, 'For this reason a man shall leave his father and mother and be joined to his wife, and the two shall become one flesh'? So then, they are no longer two but one flesh. Therefore what God has joined together, let not man separate." They said to Him, "Why then did Moses command to give a certificate of divorce, and to put her away?" He said to them, "Moses, because of the hardness of your hearts, permitted you to divorce your wives, but from the beginning it was not so. And I say to you, whoever divorces his wife, except for sexual immorality, and marries another, commits adultery; and whoever marries her who is divorced commits adultery." His disciples said to Him, "If such is the case of the man with his wife, it is better not to marry." (Matthew 19:3–10)

It is clear from this passage that a "biblical" marriage, one that conforms to the original plan of God, is a marriage that is monogamous ("one"), heterosexual ("man and woman"), and perpetual ("one flesh"). Modern attempts to "reform" marriage by permitting homosexual unions, polygamy, open marriages, or easy divorce, are clearly contrary to the revealed law of God.

Because man (Adam and Eve) was created a social and sexual being, God designed marriage to be a blessing to him, so that his emotional and physical needs might be satisfied. Moreover, God gave him a mandate to exercise dominion over the earth, and this mandate required the procreation, nurture, and education of children.

Now, because marriage is a divine institution and essential to the continuance and happiness of the human race, God has hedged it about with protective legislation. The divine purpose of the seventh commandment is to guard the institution of marriage, and thereby the family itself. *Anything that attacks marriage and family essentially assaults life itself*, for marriage is the vehicle for propagating and protecting human life. Therefore, in the Sermon on the Mount, Jesus follows the commandment against murder with the commandment against adultery, for both murder and adultery are fundamental attacks on the security and well-being of human life. Speaking of the gravity of adultery, R. L. Dabney noted:

> Its eminence in criminality is due to these traits: that in addition to the uncleanness, it involves the breach of the marriage contract, the treachery contained therein; and that by corrupting the descent of families, it uproots the whole foundation of domestic society. Adultery and divorce without cause are directly antagonistic thereto. They are therefore deadly stabs against all home affections, against all training of children, against every rudiment of social order. Were all to take the license

of the adulterer, men would in due time be reduced precisely to degradation of wild beasts. The sin of the adulterer, therefore, is scarcely less enormous than that of the murderer. The latter destroys man's temporal existence; the former destroys all that makes existence a boon.[3]

THE DANGER OF LUST

Only when we appreciate the supreme importance of marriage can we understand why Jesus suggests such a radical and painful remedy to lust.

> If your right eye causes you to sin, pluck it out and cast it from you; for it is more profitable for you that one of your members perish, than for your whole body to be cast into hell. And if your right hand causes you to sin, cut it off and cast it from you; for it is more profitable for you that one of your members perish, than for your whole body to be cast into hell. (Matthew 5:29–30)

Jesus here employs the analogy of amputation, from which we should learn several lessons that are relevant to modesty. First, He is saying, in effect: "If a man, in order to save his life, will amputate a diseased member of his body (say an eye or a hand), should he not also amputate an evil desire in order to save his soul?" Lust, being tantamount to adultery, is such a grave offense that it must be mercilessly amputated, or it will lead the soul to hell. Lust is a deadly desire.

But lust is also a destructive desire. It is clear that Jesus meant His hearers to understand that what they were justifying as legitimate divorce was really only pretence for unbridled lust. It was lust, not some fault in the spouse, that was the real motive for the divorce. But not only divorce, lust leads to sexual promiscuity, which leads to disease, abortion, and fatherless children. Lust leads to rape, sexual abuse, seduction, and incest. And lust, of course, is at the root of pornography, which feeds many of these other lusts. Surely lust is a destructive desire.

Therefore, lust requires radical surgery. Amputation is not a halfway measure. As Sinclair Ferguson said, "The consequences [of amputation] seem almost unbearable. But the drastic nature of the remedy is simply an index of the radical danger of the sin. It is not a situation for negotiation."[4] Indeed, we must be willing to deal with lust even if the operation is painful. And it probably will be.

MODESTY AND MARRIAGE

Though Jesus does not specifically mention modesty in His teaching on lust, marriage, and divorce, its relevance is plain. Marriage is a divine institution of supreme importance to the welfare of mankind, and sexual immodesty is a temptation to married men to violate their marriage vows. It is an invitation to infidelity. It is not surprising, therefore, that as our society has become more sexually "liberated"—meaning more sensual and immodest—there has been a dramatic increase in adultery. A 1998 study titled *Adultery* reported that 78 percent of British husbands have committed adultery, with similar numbers in America.[5]

Of course, a woman who dresses in a sexually provocative manner may not be thinking of seduction or adultery at all. She may only want a little attention. In fact, she might be appalled at what some men "imagine" when seeing her. If solicited for sex, she would probably reply with a slap in the face. Nevertheless, a woman must understand the language she is speaking to men. She must realize that if she dresses in a sensual way, she is unwittingly assaulting the integrity and security of marriage, because she is causing a man to look away from his wife and toward her. Many affairs have begun with a furtive glance.

In light of the value God places on marriage and fidelity, immodesty is no small sin. It is not simply a silly and vain form of self-display. It is a snare to serious sin. And for those who are married, it is a provocation to commit adultery. Anyone who understands both the high view of marriage and the high crime of adultery taught in the Bible will certainly think twice before dressing immodestly. A truly godly woman will do nothing to weaken marriage or strengthen lust. On the contrary, she rather will dress and behave modestly in order to preserve the sanctity of marriage, including her own.

Moreover, modesty relates to marriage in yet another way. The single woman in search of a lifelong marriage partner often attracts a prospective mate by her appearance. This simple fact is the basis of her obsession with fashion. But the question every young woman needs to ask is this: What kind of man am I attracting? In other words, if a woman dresses sexually to attract a man, then what kind of man will come calling? The answer is simple: The bait determines the fish. So, if a young woman really is interested in finding a spiritual partner, the last thing she should do is dress immodestly. Provocative attire will attract the wrong kind of man. As John Newton put it:

> The worst of all the fashions are those, which are evidently calculated to allure the eyes, and to draw the

attention of our [the male] sex. . . . They are indeed
noticed by the men, but not to their honour nor
advantage. The manner of their dress gives encouragement to vile and insidious men, and exposes them
to dangerous temptations. . . . But honest and sensible men regard their exterior, as a warning signal, not
to choose a companion for life, from among persons
of this light and volatile turn of mind.[6]

When it comes to finding a man, no attention is
better than the wrong attention. "What kind of persons
are those to whom you could be recommended by gay
or costly apparel?" asks Wesley. "None that are any way
likely to make you happy; this pleases only the silliest and
worst of men."[7]

A modest woman, on the other hand, is not only com-
municating her respect for the institution of marriage, she
is also telling all would-be suitors that she is not cheap.
She is valuable, and in order to "have her" the suitor must
pay the price of genuine love and lasting commitment. In
other words, male obligation is the counterpart of female
modesty. A man must earn her love by becoming worthy
of her. Wendy Shalit explains:

> The tie between this notion of male obligation and
> profound respect for female modesty is no accident,
> nor was it confined to post-Elizabethan England.
> German legend tells us the "eternal feminine"
> gives women the enduring power to spiritualize
> mankind, while the classic siren leads men to their
> destruction. These images point to a very real and
> important truth: what women will and will not
> permit does have a profound way of influencing the
> behavior of an entire society. This influence is felt

not simply because a woman has traditionally incul-
cated . . . the mores in her children and thereby
those of the next generation. A woman's sexual
modesty puts her, significantly, in a position to be
the ultimate worldly arbiter of a man's worth. . . .
Since respect for her modesty gave her the freedom
to withhold affection, so to speak, until a virtuous
man came around, men were in turn inspired to
become worthy of her.[8]

So, instead of dressing to gain carnal admirers, a spiritual young woman should adorn herself modestly and with
good works. A spiritually minded man—the kind of man
whom she would really want to marry anyway—will then
perceive her beauty and labor to earn the reward of her
virtue.

6

Robes of Righteous-
ness

To reject all idea and effort to

add the fair to the good, the

beautiful to the useful, would be

to oppose and not to imitate, . . .

the works of the Great Creator.

JOHN ANGELL JAMES

WE BEGAN OUR STUDY OF modesty with a couple of brief definitions. We defined *immodesty* as "apparel, action, or speech which is ostentatious, vain, provocative, or sensual; and which thereby reveals a carnal, worldy, or unsanctified heart." Whereas *modesty* we defined as "dressing, acting, or speaking with propriety, respect, and moderation." Cleary, modesty deals with appearance and clothing, so we must consider a Christian view of clothing, and then we can better discern how certain clothes contravene biblical norms of modesty.

THE PURPOSE OF CLOTHING

The first and most obvious use of clothing is to cover the body. This is the *moral use* of clothing. We learn in Genesis that Adam and Eve, when in a state of innocence, were naked, yet were not ashamed. After the Fall, their eyes were opened, "and they knew that they were naked; and they sewed fig leaves together and made themselves coverings" (Genesis 3: 7). The original impulse to cover themselves was rooted in a sense of sin or shame. Whatever may have been their consciousness before, they now realized that it was wrong to be naked. It was now *shameful* for their bodies to be *uncovered* for public display. That this impulse to cover themselves was essentially sound is verified by God's subsequent act of covering them with animal skins.

Another purpose of clothing is its *practical use*. While in the Garden, Adam and Eve did not need clothing due to the ideal condition of the climate. There were no extremes in temperature, no rain or snow, no burning sun or blustery winds. The weather was idyllic. Many scholars believe that the "firmament," which was created on the second day, served as a protective covering over the earth, not allowing harmful rays of the sun to reach the earth, and serving to control the climate. After the Fall, however, sin introduced disharmony even into nature as God cursed the ground for Adam's sin (Genesis 3:17). After God punished the earth with the Flood, the firmament was broken up and the climate began to change. Clothing was then needed, as it is now, to protect the body from unfavorable weather.

A third use of clothing is the *aesthetic use*. Clothes are an adornment to the body. When the apostle Paul urged Christian women to "adorn themselves in modest apparel," he was acknowledging that clothing is for adornment or enhancement. What Paul forbade was not the use of clothing for embellishment *per se*. This he took for granted. In fact, the Scripture as a whole acknowledges that beautification is a legitimate use of clothing. The desire for decoration, in fact, is an aspect of our divine image. "There is in human nature an instinctive propensity to decoration," said J. A. James. "This taste . . . is in its own nature an imitation of the workmanship of God, who, 'by his Spirit has garnished the heavens,' and covered the earth with beauty."

> Hence, I think that both the apostles [Paul and Peter] who touch on the subject of personal decoration for Christian women, are to be understood not as condemning all ornament, but only regulating it. The propensity to personal decoration is, without a doubt, peculiarly strong in the female heart. That a maid "should forget her ornaments, or a bride her attire," is spoken of by the prophet as unlikely to a proverb. There is nothing wrong in the instinct itself. It serves important purposes. Its total absence is felt as a serious interruption to the pleasure of social intercourse. A sloven is disagreeable; a slattern intolerable. Christianity makes not war on any of man's natural propensities, but only on their abuse. Its object is not to eradicate our instincts, but to prune and train them, and make them bear good fruit.[1]

There is nothing wrong with a woman (or a man) wanting to dress in a way that enhances appearance. But a question immediately comes to mind: What is the motive? Yes, it is morally acceptable to dress in an attractive fashion, but what is going on inside? Are you driven by insecurity? Are you craving attention? Are you vain?

A final use of clothing could be called the *religious use*. We see in Scripture that God provided an elaborate wardrobe for the priesthood. Their clothing was important because of its symbolic value. Each piece of their uniform served as an object lesson of an important spiritual truth.

IMMODEST DRESS

One way to discuss what is acceptable clothing is to mention those things that are breaches of modesty, that is, clothing that is not consistent with the above purposes. While this approach may seem negative, it is the same approach used by the artist creating a sculpture: the ugly parts of the marble block are chiseled away until what is left standing reflects the artist's conception of beauty. We must remember, however, that our goal here is not necessarily to provide a list of prohibited articles of dress. Instead, we are trying to provide boundaries and principles.

Ostentation

Ostentation is the problem of "too much," that is, elaborate or extravagant display. Ostentation is marked by a conspicuous, vainglorious, and sometimes pretentious display, and may apply to clothing, hair, jewelry, or cosmetics. In 1 Timothy 2:9, the main problem addressed by Paul is the extravagant custom of decking the hair with jewelry. According to Barnes, "Females in the East pay much more attention to the hair than is commonly done with us. It is plaited with great care, and arranged in various forms, according to the prevailing fashion, and often ornamented with spangles or with silver wire or tissue interwoven."[2]

Apparel (including hairstyles or jewelry) that is strange, bizarre, or "shocking" is by definition ostentatious. One has only to browse through a contemporary fashion magazine to see the most strange and flamboyant outfits. And if a Christian woman struts into church looking like she just stepped out of *Vogue*, or if a Christian teen shows up with a purple Mohawk, then we have a problem with ostentation.

Ostentation is sinful because its goal (whether admitted or not) is to be different or exceptional in order to attract attention. It is wanting to be on center stage, to have top billing, to be noticed. It's really all about self. A Christian woman who loves Christ, however, will not be seeking attention or glory for herself. On the contrary, she will strive to honor and exalt the Lord in all that she does. Her motto will be: "He must increase, but I must decrease" (John 3:30).

✑*Androgyny*

Another breach of modesty is androgyny, which means clothing having the characteristics or nature of both male and female. By androgyny, traditional male and female roles are obscured or reversed. When Paul exhorted Christian women to be modest, however, he was not telling them to dress like men. On the contrary, androgynous apparel, like ostentation, is equally a violation of biblical standards of modesty. For instance: "A woman shall not wear anything that pertains to a man, nor shall a man put on a woman's garment, for all who do so are an abomination to the LORD your God" (Deuteronomy 22:5).

Or look at Paul's teaching on the distinction of the sexes, which was rooted in nature, not custom.

> Now I praise you, brethren, that you remember me
> in all things and keep the traditions just as I delivered
> them to you. But I want you to know that the

head of every man is Christ, the head of woman
is man, and the head of Christ is God. Every man
praying or prophesying, having his head covered,
dishonors his head. But every woman who prays or
prophesies with her head uncovered dishonors her
head, for that is one and the same as if her head were
shaved. For if a woman is not covered, let her also be
shorn. But if it is shameful for a woman to be shorn
or shaved, let her be covered. For a man indeed
ought not to cover his head, since he is the image
and glory of God; but woman is the glory of man.
For man is not from woman, but woman from man.
Nor was man created for the woman, but woman
for the man. For this reason the woman ought to
have a symbol of authority on her head, because of
the angels. Nevertheless, neither is man independent of woman, nor woman independent of man,
in the Lord. For as woman came from man, even so
man also comes through woman; but all things are
from God. Judge among yourselves. Is it proper for
a woman to pray to God with her head uncovered?
Does not even nature itself teach you that if a man
has long hair, it is a dishonor to him? But if a woman
has long hair, it is a glory to her; for her hair is given
to her for a covering. But if anyone seems to be
contentious, we have no such custom, nor do the
churches of God. (1 Corinthians 11:2–16)

It is clear from these two passages alone that men and
women are not only different, but that they are required
to look or appear different. The rationale for these commands is a basic fact of creation: male and female are
fixed types of the created order that we must not confuse
or blur. We must "live out," as it were, the truth of God's

creation. We are living symbols of the divine archetype in creation. We cannot change our gender, nor even *appear* to change our gender, without revolting against our Maker. As Douglas Wilson said, "The Bible prohibits, in the strongest language, the kind of sexual confusion which would result in a woman wearing a man's clothing or a man wearing a woman's clothing. To be guilty of confusion on that point is to be guilty of an abomination."[3]

In our day, the problem of androgyny works both ways—men dressing like women, and women dressing like men. While some of this is motivated by nothing more than the desire to "shock," the more serious issue is our culture's rejection of the biblical doctrine of creation. If God did not create the world and make man and woman in His image, then we can make them in our image. We can manipulate not only appearance, but even our gender. We can be our own creator. We can be a god, the ultimate act of rebellion.

In the church we honor and profess God's created order by how we dress. We submit to our creaturehood. We glory both in masculinity and in femininity. We do not ask women to be plain and ugly by wearing potato sacks. We would have them adorn their femininity and not conform to the world's attempt to transform them into men. Our men, on the other hand, must resist every attempt to tame and emasculate them, even in their appearance.

⸱Sensuality
Sensuality consists in the gratification of the senses or the indulgence of the physical appetites. When we say that someone is sensual, we mean that they are devoted to

or preoccupied with the senses or appetites. There is no better definition of sensuality than the one given by the apostle John: "For all that is in the world—the lust of the flesh, the lust of the eyes, and the pride of life—is not of the Father but is of the world. And the world is passing away, and the lust of it; but he who does the will of God abides forever" (1 John 2:16–17).

Clothing is sensual or provocative when it is either "too little," "too thin," or "too tight." By "too little" we mean things like short skirts or shorts, low-cut hip-huggers, blouses that are either too short (halter tops), unbuttoned, or too low-cut; gaping holes on sleeveless shirts that expose the undergarments or breasts, and things similar to this. There are too many examples to mention but the basic idea is that the article of clothing is leaving too much flesh exposed.

There is also the problem of "too thin," which means sheer or see-through clothing. Many blouses, sweaters, and even dresses are designed to be sheer enough for the body or underwear to be seen. This is not an accident. It is by design. But if a person can see through your clothes, then you have defeated the very purpose of clothing, which is to cover what is underneath! A woman who is bold enough to wear sheer clothing ought to be brave enough to discard it. For it is all the same to the male observer.

Sensual clothing is also "too tight." Indeed, many female fashions are intentionally designed in such a way as to accentuate and flatter the female form. One way this is accomplished is by cutting the pants or blouse to fit extremely tightly in order to draw the eye to the erotic zones of the body. It is not just "exposed flesh" that arouses a man's lust, however. It is the female "form."

Fashion designers understand this and have made clothing "too tight" in order to accentuate and highlight a woman's shape. So, clothing that is "too tight" may cover the body in one sense, but in another sense it makes the body even more visible and alluring, even without showing an inch of flesh. Jeff Pollard explains it like this:

> Let's face it: packaging is generally far more erotic than raw nudity. Alison Lurie, author of *The Language of Clothing*, observes that "some modern writers believe that the deliberated concealment of certain parts of the body originated not as a way of discouraging sexual interest, but as a clever device for arousing it. According to this view, clothes are the physical equivalent of remarks like 'I've got a secret'; they are a tease, a come-on. It is certainly true that parts of the human form considered sexually arousing are often covered in such a way as to exaggerate or draw attention to them." Kidwell and Steele add that "clothes are especially sexy when they call attention to the naked body underneath." Every human being that is even slightly aware of his or her sexuality knows this. . . . The fashion industry does not believe that the principle purpose of clothing is to cover the body; it believes that the principle purpose of clothing is *sexual attraction*. This is the very opposite of Christian modesty.[4]

Pollard later states:

> Being drawn to a person's God-given beauty is one thing; having one's eyes *directed* to another's body by a sensually *designed* garment is another. While clothing does not have to smother one's gender, any apparel designed to draw the eye to the erotic zones

93

of the body cannot fill the requirement for Biblical decency. The shapes of men and women's bodies are *not* evil; they were designed by a *good* Creator, Who pronounced them *good*. . . . Garments, like all material things, are not sinful in and of themselves. But exposing or sensually packaging the body, while provoking lust in others' fallen flesh, is.[5]

Association

One of the more subtle forms of immodesty creeping into the church is the problem of association. Association occurs when something is linked in memory or imagination with a different thing or person. It is the process of forming mental connections or bonds between sensations, ideas, or memories.

Perhaps the best example is brand-name clothing. Brands often have a "message" or "image" associated with them, and when we wear that brand (with the brand name exposed as it often is), we are both endorsing the image and calling up that image in other people's minds. A glaring example of this is Abercrombie & Fitch clothing. Most people (especially young people) know that A&F has produced a clothing catalog displaying male and female nudity. Essentially, their catalog is a "soft porn" magazine.[6] So, if a young woman walks into church with the name Abercrombie & Fitch emblazoned across the front of her shirt, (across the front of her breasts no less), what are the young men going to think? What signal is she sending? Well, if she isn't aware of A&F propaganda, she is telling us she is clueless. And if she is aware, then she is telling us she is loose. She is sending sensual signals by association. Another company that has made the headlines is Calvin Klein. Their clothing ads are basically explicit commercials for teenage promiscuity. Even *Playboy* has gotten into the act and now has a clothing line displaying their trademark bunny. It is not possible for a man to see this symbol without thinking of pornography. Is that what a Christian woman wants men to think of when they see her?

The principle of association can apply to styles as well as brand names. Some articles of clothing may be innocent in themselves, yet due to association they send the wrong message. How many young Christian teens are dressing like Britney? Yet Britney is clearly selling sex, not music. Or how about a simple item like a black leather collar? In itself it's harmless, but when put in its social context it conjures up images of the Goth subculture, which is nihilistic, brutish, and violent. Or what of the young man who wears an earring? Is he intending to endorse male effeminacy or even homosexuality? The point here is not to simply prohibit certain brands or styles. Instead, we must recognize that our clothing often sends messages, and that we are responsible for what our clothes are "saying." As one author put it, "Even if an item of clothing is not intrinsically immodest, it can still function as a durable symbol of vice when invested with negative meaning by culture."[7]

PRINCIPLES OF APPAREL

It should be clear from what has been said that some types of clothing are not appropriate for Christian women. Of course, there is much room for personal preferences and tastes. Indeed, there may be enough room for disagreement when it comes to actual practice versus theory. But we should all be able to agree on a few things.

First, one of the primary purposes of clothing is to cover nakedness. But as we have seen, this may also mean more than just covering the flesh. When evaluating her wardrobe, a Christian woman must take into account the modern fashion industry's attempt to accent the female shape, including the erotic zones. In a word, could the clothes in question be characterized as "sexy"? If so, then they are clothes that don't clothe, coverings that don't cover. Skimpy, tight, and sheer apparel won't do the job of covering nakedness.

Also (and this relates to the first point), a Christian woman should not wear anything that causes others to stumble. We will discuss this more at length later, but for now we only mention that as Christians we must walk in love toward one another. And if certain articles of clothing cause a man to lust, then the loving thing is to avoid that clothing.

Third, a Christian woman should not wear anything designed to bring attention to herself. That means any apparel that is shocking or bizarre, even if it is sexually modest. Her goal ought to be to honor Christ, not herself. This is really a matter of the heart, which we will discuss shortly. But clearly ostentation is a very visible sign that a woman is seeking attention. Plainness, not ugliness, is next to godliness.

Fourth, a Christian woman should not be "preoccupied" with her appearance. This is actually the primary point that both Paul (1 Timothy 2) and Peter (1 Peter 3) tried to impress on Christian women. It is lawful to adorn and beautify one's appearance, but don't be obsessed with how you look. Barnes has given the true meaning:

> It may be a difficult question to settle how much

ornament is allowable, and when the true line is passed. But though this cannot be settled by any exact rule, since much must depend on age, and on the relative rank in life, and the means which one may possess; yet there is one general rule which is applicable to all, and which might regulate all. It is, that the true line is passed when more is thought of this external adorning, than the ornament of the heart. Any external decoration which occupies the mind, and which engrosses the time and attention more than the virtues of the heart, we may be certain is wrong.[8]

Give more attention to the inner person than the outer person. Be more concerned about the beauty of your soul than the appearance of your body.

In addition, a Christian woman should understand that she is wearing or adorning the gospel. In 1 Timothy 2: 9–10, the contrast is not primarily between two types of clothing. It is between two types of adornment—one of clothing, the other of good works. When a woman professes godliness, that profession must be matched by her appearance and behavior. And to profess godliness means being more concerned about good works than good looks. As J. A. James said:

> Study your profession, and thoroughly understand what it implies and enjoins. Consider well what sanctity of conduct; what spirituality of mind; what separation from the world in spirit and taste; what devotional feelings; what faith, hope, love, and humility; what amiableness of disposition and amenity of temper, are included in the declaration (and that declaration you have actually made), "I

am a Christian." You should not have made such a profession if you did not understand it, or mean to sustain it. I must remind you, it is a solemn thing to profess to be a disciple of Christ."[9]

Godliness is devotion to God in Christ as our supreme love; a love more intense than our desire for earthly fads or fashions. When a woman adorns the gospel, everything about her reflects on her Lord.

Last, when evaluating the contents of your closet, here is a good general rule: When in doubt throw it out. It is always better to be safe than sorry. Look at the bright side: you now have a good excuse to get a new wardrobe!

7

Women Professing Godliness

Since the disposition of the inner man is principally manifest in the countenance, the speech, and the apparel, therefore the behavior may be tried by these, whether it is according to holiness or not.

THOMAS TAYLOR

WHENEVER YOU MENTION THE WORD *modesty*, people almost always think of clothes. On one occasion we were speaking at a home education conference, and after a session we mentioned in a conversation that we were writing a book on modesty. The woman we were in conversation with looked mildly uncomfortable, ignored the comment, and continued to talk. Sometime later in the day that same woman came up to us with an embarrassed look and said, "Do you think I'm *dressed* okay?"

As we have seen, attire is a significant part of modesty. But that is not all. Biblical modesty transcends clothing and pertains also to our demeanor, that is, our actions and conduct. Our conduct is, of course, ultimately rooted in the state of our hearts. The two are inseparable.

DECENT DEPORTMENT

There are three ways we might violate biblical modesty in our demeanor. The first is called *deportment*, which is the way one behaves or one's bearing. As it relates to modesty, deportment has to do with things like walking rather than "strutting." A woman may walk in such a way that she brings attention to herself, especially to her breasts or buttocks. This is, of course, provocative and sensual. The prophet Isaiah described this well:

> Moreover the LORD says:
>> "Because the daughters of Zion are haughty,
>> And walk with outstretched necks
>> And wanton eyes,
>> Walking and mincing as they go,
>> Making a jingling with their feet,
>> Therefore the Lord will strike with a scab
>> The crown of the head of the daughters of
>>> Zion,
>> And the LORD will uncover their secret parts."
>> (Isaiah 3:16–17)

Also, women should be conscious to sit and cross their legs modestly, even if wearing pants. They should learn to bend down and not bend over. They should be aware of any body positions that might expose any part of their undergarments.

Both men and women should also be mindful to keep their hands to themselves. Being "touchy" with the opposite sex is courting trouble. A warm handshake is acceptable; a warm hug is not. Rarely should a married man embrace another woman. And if a woman does hug another man, she should be conscious not to press herself against his body. As Frances Benton said: "A well-mannered man avoids touching a woman unnecessarily. . . . The line between friendship and pawing is a very fine one."[1]

Likewise, men and women who are not married should not be alone together for any length of time. Manis Friedman has given the following wise advice:

> It is preferable that a man and woman who are not married to one another, and are not members of the same family, avoid being alone together in a closed room. This doesn't mean they shouldn't be friends or coworkers. But they need to take into consideration that whenever a man and a woman have a friendship or a working relationship, it will have a potentially sexual component. For this reason they should follow certain precautions.[2]

While all may be innocent, we are required to avoid even the appearance of evil. Spending time privately with the opposite sex is a temptation to sin and a sure way to mar your reputation. This rule applies even to the pastor who may have to counsel a woman. If so, he should have present either his wife or the counselee's husband.

THE TAMED TONGUE

Second, we must be modest in our *words*. *What* is spoken; *how* it is spoken; and *to whom* it is spoken, are three considerations relative to modesty. In Ephesians 5 we are told:

> But fornication and all uncleanness or covetousness, let it not even be named among you, as is fitting for saints; neither filthiness, nor foolish talking, nor coarse jesting, which are not fitting, but rather giving of thanks. For this you know, that no fornicator, unclean person, nor covetous man, who is an idola-

ter, has any inheritance in the kingdom of Christ and God. Let no one deceive you with empty words, for because of these things the wrath of God comes upon the sons of disobedience. Therefore do not be partakers with them. For you were once darkness, but now you are light in the Lord. Walk as children of light (for the fruit of the Spirit is in all goodness, righteousness, and truth), finding out what is acceptable to the Lord. And have no fellowship with the unfruitful works of darkness, but rather expose them. For it is shameful even to speak of those things which are done by them in secret. But all things that are exposed are made manifest by the light, for whatever makes manifest is light. Therefore He says:

"Awake, you who sleep,
Arise from the dead,
And Christ will give you light."
(Ephesians 5:3–14)

Of course, lewd or sensual talk is here forbidden. Dirty jokes, as they are called, are not funny. Anything "off-color" should be avoided, especially when in mixed company. We should never suggest anything impure, sensual, or base. All that we say should have the scent of grace and gratitude upon it. "And whatever you do *in word* or deed, do all in the name of the Lord Jesus, giving thanks to God the Father through Him" (Colossians 3:17). If what you have to say could not be spoken in God's presence, it is better left unsaid.

Many things innocently and commonly spoken in mixed company need to be reconsidered. For instance, when a woman is pregnant and nearing delivery it is not uncommon for friends, both male and female, to discuss aspects of her anatomy. Another example is for a person to mention in mixed company things like bathing or dressing. "Oh, sorry I'm late for church; I lost track of time while in the shower." Statements like this paint a visual image that sticks in a person's mind. (Do you really want men thinking of you in the shower?) We must also be careful in complimenting the opposite sex. To say, "That is a nice dress," may be acceptable. But to say, "You look great," is flirtatious.

When it comes to modest speech, two general rules are helpful. One is, think before you speak. Remember, words are like plucked feathers. Once cast to the wind they can't be recovered. And second, intimate matters should stay at home. Friedman is right to say that a man and a woman who are not married "should avoid talking about intimate subjects. . . . They can discuss politics, art, business, or sports but should avoid topics that may initiate or strengthen feelings of sexuality."[3] The best policy is always to err on the side of reserve. The wise person studies how to answer.

THE LIGHT OF THE EYES

The third aspect of demeanor is looks or *countenance*. The Scripture speaks of "wanton eyes" and "eyes full of adultery." In Proverbs we read of the harlot whose "mouth drips with honey," and who "flatters with her eyes." These and other passages teach us that even if dressed modestly we can still send an immodest message by our facial expressions. It is no doubt possible to flirt without saying a word. The light in the eyes speaks volumes. A "wink of the eye" may be as sinful as a sheer skirt; an "inviting smile" as a provocative pose. Modern media provide us with plentiful examples of the haughty look and sensual gaze. Without a word, the look says it all: "I'm hot, so come and get it."

To provide guidelines of demeanor for every situation would require writing a book on etiquette, a practice that used to be common but has fallen out of fashion. For the Christian woman, however, a couple of suggestions may be helpful.

The first is to remember that as a Christian you are a representative. Because you bear the name of Christ, how you act and what you say communicate a message that will be associated with Christ. When someone interacts with you, they should get a sense of what Christ is like. Thus, the apostle Paul said, "Now thanks be to God who always leads us in triumph in Christ, and through us diffuses the fragrance of His knowledge in every place. For we are to God the fragrance of Christ among those who are being saved and among those who are perishing" (2 Corinthians 2:14–15). So, does your behavior honor Him? Are you acting in a way that causes others to reverence the name of Christ?

And second, you must always be conscious of how your behavior impacts others. Not only are you setting an example of what is acceptable Christian behavior, but as a woman you may unwittingly be proving a temptation to men. You are called to walk in love, so be considerate of others. Since men are visually stimulated so easily, dressing immodestly is a form of sexual harassment of men. Make it easier for them *not* to look.

Third, no area of your testimony should be marred by even the appearance of evil. As John Newton rightly said: "We are required to attend to things that are lovely and of good report. Every willful deviation from this rule is sinful. Why should a godly woman, or one who wishes to be thought so, make herself ridiculous, or hazard a suspicion on her character, to please and imitate an ungodly world?"[4]

The best rule of all, and the one which covers every case, is well expressed by John Wesley:

> Let a single intention to please God prescribe
> both what clothing you shall buy, and the manner
> wherein it shall be made, and how you shall put
> on and wear it. To express the same thing in other
> words: Let all you do, in this respect, be so done
> that you may offer it to God, a sacrifice accept-
> able through Christ Jesus; so that, consequently, it
> may increase your reward and brighten your crown
> in heaven. And so it will do, if it be agreeable to
> Christian humility, seriousness, and charity.[5]

8

The Hidden Person of the Heart

Yet we must always begin with the dispositions; for where debauchery reigns within, there will be no modesty in the outward dress.

JOHN CALVIN

WHILE PREPARING *THE BEAUTY OF MODESTY*, we did an informal survey of some women whom we respect. The question we asked them was: "Why would a Christian woman dress immodestly?" Their answers, which we will give in a moment, surprised us. But here are a few possible answers.

MODESTY AND DESIRE

One possible answer could be simple ignorance or naiveté. Perhaps an immodest woman just doesn't understand that skintight jeans and cleavage cause men to look—and to lust. While hard to believe, this lack of understanding could occur, especially when the "woman" is a teenager who is just beginning to develop. While her body is "blossoming," she may not yet realize exactly why she all of a sudden is getting so much male attention. This type of ignorance, however, is neither harmless nor excusable. Lust does great harm, as we have seen, and women are responsible for not enticing others to lust. Moreover, Christian parents, especially fathers, have a moral duty to instruct their daughters in appropriate dress. There is really no good reason why a young woman from a Christian home should be dressing in a bizarre or provocative way.

But what about the adult woman, whether single or married, who is ostentatious or exposing too much flesh? Is she simply ignorant? Well, when we did our unscientific survey, we were struck by the fact that every woman we asked said the same thing: *"An immodest woman knows exactly what she is doing. She wants attention."* If this is true, then a woman who intentionally dresses immodestly has one or more of the following problems: insecurity, vanity, or sensuality.

A woman who is looking for attention has an emotional deficit of some sort. She is insecure and thus needs male attention to feel valued. If we are talking about a teenage girl, then the real problem is probably that she is craving the male attention she is not receiving from her father. In the case of a married woman, she is inadvertently advertising the dismal state of her marriage. It is generally true that the motive for promiscuity differs according to gender: men are looking for sex, and women are looking for love. So when a woman dresses immodestly, she may be acting out of an emotional desire to feel loved, valued, or secure. In other words, there is a problem somewhere in the home.

Yet the deeper problem is spiritual. Though God provides a spouse or parent to love us and nurture our sense of value, ultimately our sense of worth must come from our relationship with Christ. What demonstrates to us the love of God more than the Cross? Could He do any more? Give any more? How valuable is the human soul—how valuable is *your soul*—when measured by the gauge of Christ's sufferings? How precious must we be to God, seeing He gave the precious blood of Christ to redeem us? Thus, there is no need to find our sense of value in the opinion of others, when we know—and we mean *really know*—that God loves us.

Another possible problem is vanity, which is an expression of selfishness or self-centeredness. It is, according to Wesley, "the love and desire of being admired and praised."[1] Thus it is that many women (and men) dress with an eye toward public opinion and public praise. The world becomes their stage, and they aspire to be at the center. What makes vanity different from insecurity is that the vain person is craving admiration out of pride. A vain woman really does believe that she is beautiful (whether she is or not). She is "flaunting her stuff" precisely because she thinks she has it to flaunt. The turning heads stroke her pride. With each glance her ego swells.

Nothing could be more contrary to Christian humility, of course. In fact, vanity is not a petty vice at all. It is, notes Robert Hall, "destructive to society." Why? Because vanity "forms the heart to such a profound indifference to the welfare of others, that . . . you will infallibly find the vain man is his own center. Attentive only to himself . . . he considers life as a stage on which he is performing a part, and mankind in no other light than spectators."[2] In other words, the vain person demeans other people by valuing them only for the praise they can offer at the altar of his vanity. It is, therefore, profoundly selfish and fundamentally antisocial. The vain woman is too in love with herself to love anyone else.

In fact, according to Shalit, the essence of immodesty is the "desire for spectators." She explains: "Bathsheba's immodesty was typically conveyed [in Western art] by depicting her *enjoying the spectators*, particularly King David, at her bath. Many fifteenth-century woodcuts show Bathsheba sometimes dressed and sometimes not. It was something entirely independent of dress, namely her desire for spectators, which betrayed her immodesty."[3]

A third problem may be carnality or sensuality. Of course, vanity is a symptom of an unsanctified heart, but the carnality we have in mind here is more specifically sexual or sensual in nature. Since we live in a pornographic and promiscuous society, many men and women converted as adults enter the church with sexual baggage. Any pastor could tell you just how broken people can be from sexual abuse and promiscuity. And some women who are recent converts are still in need of sanctification in dress, demeanor, and desire. Some people, especially those who were either exposed to pornography or sexually abused at a young age, struggle for many years to gain freedom from sexual bondage, acting out, and lust.

A Sanctified Heart

As we have been saying all along, we cannot separate the internal and external. The root issue is the heart, and what is in the heart usually works its way into every area of our lives. So, it is not possible to accurately explain proper dress or demeanor without also discussing the virtuous heart, for out of it flow the issues of life.

When we look in the New Testament there are

several terms used to describe proper female modesty. One such term is *aidos*, found in 1 Timothy 2:9, which is variously translated as "propriety," "shamefastness," and "decency," among other English words. In Classical Greek, the term had reference to a sense of awe or reverence for that which is sacred. In contrast to pride, it signified "a respect for the established sacred institutions (e.g., home, marriage, laws of hospitality), or for the privileges of certain people (e.g., king, priest, orator, etc.), in the sense of piety. . . . It also connotes anxious avoidance, in the sense of fear of any damage or change to existing circumstances."[4] The only other occurrence in the New Testament is in Hebrews 12:28: "Let us have grace, by which we may serve God acceptably with reverence and godly fear."

Thus, a modest woman is anxious to not harm the institution of marriage by dishonoring her husband or tempting others. Moreover, in the Christian assembly (which is the context of 1 Timothy 2:9–10), she displays reverence for God by her demeanor and dress. The Lutheran scholar Lenski says that *aidos* suggests "the negative side of the moral sensibility which shrinks from transgressing the limits of propriety," while R. C. Trench notes that *aidos* is "the tendency which shrinks from overpassing the limits of womanly reserve and modesty, as well as the dishonor which would justly attach thereto."[5]

One author, writing in the 1950s, talked of modesty being a matter of appropriateness:

> Specific rules about modesty change with the styles. Our Victorian ancestors, for instance, would judge us utterly depraved for wearing the modern bathing

suit. Real modesty, however, is a constant and desirable quality. It is based not on fashion but on appropriateness. A woman boarding a subway in shorts at the rush hour is immodest not because the shorts are in themselves indecent, but because they are worn in the wrong place at the wrong time. A well-mannered and self-respecting woman avoids clothes and behavior that are inappropriate or conspicuous.[6]

In the original Authorized Version of the Bible (popularly called the King James Version), the translation of *aidos* is "shamefastness," which was mistakenly changed to the current "shamefacedness." What "shamefastness" captures is the idea of not doing what is shameful, out of an inner sense of what is reverent, honorable, or respectable. When we say someone's behavior is "shameless," we mean they have no sense of shame, and thus are given to inappropriate or disgusting behavior. A woman who has *aidos* has a sense of shame, which is another way of saying that she has self-respect. She has too much respect for herself to act or dress in a shameful way.

But she also has too much respect for others to treat them in a shameful way. As Frances Benton said:

> Another expression of our basic consideration of others is how we act in public. Exhibitionism is bad manners, not only because it is immodest but because it is inconsiderate. A lady or gentleman, therefore, does not wear outlandish clothes on a city street, or carry on an embarrassingly personal conversation in a crowded elevator. We don't spit our germs onto sidewalks, or cough our colds into other people's faces. Needless to say, it is not a pretty sight, either, to see someone combing his hair, pick-

ing his teeth, or cleaning his nails in public. It is not
good manners—because it is not considerate—to
do anything in public that might annoy, embarrass,
disgust, or inconvenience other people.[7]

Another important term also found in 1 Timothy
is *sophrosynes*, which can be translated as "discretion,"
"sobriety," or "moderation." *Sophrosynes* belongs to a word
group that suggests the idea of being reasonable, sensible,
or prudent. It comes from *sophron*, which is a combina-
tion of *sos* (safe, sound) and *phren* (the heart as the seat
of the passions). As developed by the Stoics, *sophrosynes*
included such subordinate virtues as discipline, decency,
propriety, modesty, temperance, and self-control.[8]

A woman who possesses the virtue of *sophrosynes* has
"that habitual inner self-government, with its constant
rein on all the passions and desires."[9] She is self-controlled,
and thus does not give in to the desire for attention and
praise. As Lenski has rightly noted, "Vanity, pride and
other improprieties are here excluded." And whereas
"extravagant dress is generally worn for mere display with
the secret desire to produce envy," the prudent woman
is able to control her passions.[10] Because she has a strong
inner discipline, she is able to resist the risings of pride.
Her modest dress is a fitting picture of her mortified desire.

In Titus chapter 2, the older women are told to
instruct the younger women to be "discreet" (*sophrosynes*)
and "chaste" (*hagnes*). (The former word is the same as in
1 Timothy. The latter word, *chaste*, is also found in 1 Peter
3:2, where Peter echoes Paul's call to modesty.) According
to Thomas Taylor, the puritan expositor of Titus, the grace
of discretion "requires that the reins of affections be subject

unto reason and judgment, and that no thought be allowed to settle in the mind which is not first warranted in the Word. . . . This grace is then the watchman and moderator of the mind, keeping and guarding it from unlawful pleasures, and in lawful pleasures curbing and cutting off abuse and excess. It also watches over the affections of the heart and actions of the life, resisting all light behavior, all childish carriage, and all boisterous and troublesome passions."[11]

To be "chaste" means to be pure or holy. Originally, *hagnes* was used for the attribute of deity, and then for that which inspired reverence. As it is used in 2 Corinthians 11:2 and Titus 2:5, hagnes means "chastity" or "sexual purity." To quote Taylor again: "It is a purity both of soul and body, in regard to unchaste lusts; it abandons all unlawful and strange pleasures."

> This chastity, then, is moral purity, especially as it applies to sexual desire and temptation. And it ought to manifest itself "in a modest countenance; in a chaste ear, not entertaining impure communication; and in a pure tongue, by grave and holy speech, exempt from lightness and rottenness."[12]

Immodest dress is the antithesis of the purity required of Christian women, especially dress that is in any way seductive, such as revealing the breasts or midriff. The pure woman will not only be pure in her own thoughts, but she will not tempt others to be impure in their thoughts. While dressing to be attractive, she will not dress to be "sexy."

Moreover, older women themselves are to be models for the younger by being "reverent in behavior," or as the Authorized Version states, "that they be in behavior as becometh holiness" (Titus 2:3). The term "behavior" (*katastemati*) means in the original "mien, demeanor, or deportment, including . . . the movements of the body, the expression of the countenance, what is said, and what is left unsaid. The whole habit and composition or structure of mind and body." . . . Thus, "behavior" includes both the inner and outer person, and both ought to be "reverent" or sacred. It is the kind of behavior that naturally and easily inspires respect.[13]

The well-known church father Jerome put it like this: "The women are, like the older men, to be honest, sober, chaste, strong in faith and charity and patience. They are also to bear themselves in a way proper for their sex, to maintain a holy manner in bodily movements, facial expressions, words, silence, and whatever tends to the dignity of a holy decorum."[14] Commenting on this verse, Calvin judiciously noticed that "reverent behavior" applies to female dress as well as actions. "We very frequently see, that females advanced in age either continue to dress with the lightness of youthful years, or have something superstitious in their apparel, and seldom hit the golden mean. Paul wished to guard against both extremes, by enjoining them to follow a course that is agreeable both to outward propriety and to religion; or, if you choose to express it in simpler language, to give evidence, by their dress, that they are holy and godly women."[15]

In sum, the heart attitude is preeminent and pervasive. As goes the heart, so goes the life. And if a Christian woman has the inner qualities of self-control, discretion, purity, and holiness, her entire life will display them. As the poet George Herbert eloquently said:

Let thy mind's sweetness have its operation
Upon thy person, clothes, and habitation.[16]

Thus, the critical step in cultivating modesty is to cultivate the heart. As a Christian woman nurtures her relationship with Christ and grows in grace and knowledge, she will also be nurturing the virtue of modesty.

III

The Nurture of Modesty

From the day a girl first opens a fashion magazine until the day she dies, clothes are a major topic of discussion.

BARBARA HUGES, *DISCIPLINES OF A GODLY WOMAN*

For the wise men of old, the cardinal problem of human life was how to conform the soul to objective reality, and the solution was wisdom, self-discipline, and virtue. For the modern, the cardinal problem is how to conform reality to the wishes of man, and the solution is technique.

C. S. LEWIS QUOTED IN *THE PILLARS OF LEADERSHIP*

When religion falls low among parents, and those in the place of parents having the training up of youth in their hands, it can hardly miss to sink among the children and youth; so that if the one be bad, the other just needs be worse, except where sovereign grace interposes, and hinders the native effect of the neglect and ill example.

THOMAS BOSTON, *THE COMPLETE WORKS OF THOMAS BOSTON*

9
Hearth
and
Home

The first great task confronting

parents today is to bring their

children up within the covenant,

and in such a way as their chil-

dren feel a lifelong loyalty to that

covenant.

DOUGLAS WILSON

THE HOME IS THE CHILD'S most important moral influence. It is the child's first nursery for play, first school
for education, and first church for worship. The lessons
learned there will make an indelible mark on the child's
character—for good or for evil. As J. C. Ryle has noted,
"Early habits (if I may so speak) are everything with us,
under God. We are made what we are by training. Our
character takes the form of that mold into which our first
years are cast. . . . Time will show, I suspect, how much
we all owe to the early impressions, and how many things
in us may be traced up to seeds sown in the days of our
very infancy, by those who were about us."[1] Richard Cecil
agreed: "He has seen but little of life who does not discern
everywhere the effect of education on men's opinions and
habits of thinking. The children bring out of the nursery
that which displays itself throughout their lives."[2] So as we

consider the nurture of modesty, we have to consider the profound influence of the home and parental training.

The Family in Focus

Before discussing the parents' role in nurturing virtue, it might be wise to first mention the biblical view of the form and function of the family. As much as we would like to assume that all Evangelicals are pretty much agreed on the meaning of family, that is an assumption which is no longer safe to make. So, just for the sake of clarity, we'll first give what we believe to be the Christian definition of the family.

First, we will define marriage. According to the Scripture, marriage is a civil institution resulting from the mystical union of one man and one woman in the perpetual, covenantal relationship wherein the husband serves as the federal head of the family.

A Christian marriage is mystical. It is not a simple partnership. Nor is it a simple arrangement to cohabitate. Rather, in marriage there is a mystical or spiritual union that results in the creation of a new entity—a separate and distinct "one-flesh" family. The intimacy of the one-flesh union is such that the apostle Paul said that if a man loves his wife, then he really loves his own body (Ephesians 5:28).

A Christian marriage is heterosexual. In Matthew chapter 19, Jesus teaches on marriage and divorce and clearly articulates a heterosexual view of marriage. One *man* and one *woman* are to be joined together to form one flesh. He does not say one person and one other person; not one man and another man; but one man and one woman.

A Christian marriage is monogamous. The term *mono* means "one." God took *one* man and *one* woman and made of them *one* flesh. Thus a Christian marriage excludes polygamy, adultery, and incest. Being monogamous means being sexually content with one's spouse, and thus would also exclude the use of pornography.

A Christian marriage is also perpetual. By perpetual we mean "lifelong." In the Scripture, marriage is intended to last until one of the parties dies, or until the dissolution of the marriage through a lawful (as defined by Scripture) divorce. Adultery and desertion have always been understood to be lawful grounds for divorce.

A Christian marriage is federal. The word *federal* is derived from a Latin term that means "covenant." A biblical marriage is more than a civil contract. It is a covenant, which means that it requires both parties be of the same faith or worship the same God. The vows made at a wedding ceremony are covenantal in nature, for they morally bind the parties before God. Thus, mixed marriages are forbidden of Christians (2 Corinthians 6:14; Deuteronomy 7:1–4). However, in the case of a post-marriage conversion, a mixed marriage is not to be abandoned by the believing spouse (1 Corinthians 7:10ff.).

God ordained the family for several purposes. One is the task of dominion.

> Then God said, "Let Us make man in Our image, according to Our likeness; let them have dominion over the fish of the sea, over the birds of the air, and over the cattle, over all the earth and over every creeping thing that creeps on the earth." So God created man in His own image; in the image of God He created him; male and female He created them. Then God blessed them, and God said to them, "Be fruitful and multiply; fill the earth and subdue

it; have dominion over the fish of the sea, over the
birds of the air, and over every living thing that
moves on the earth." (Genesis 1:26–28)

This is the mandate to "subdue the earth," which is
the divine Magna Carta for all true scientific and material
progress. Man began with a mind that was perfect in its
finite capacity for learning, but he did not begin knowing
all the secrets of the universe. This "Cultural Mandate," as
it has been called, meant acquiring a knowledge and mas-
tery over his material environment, in order to bring its
elements into the service of both God and man. In fulfilling this mandate man acts as both a ruler and a creator,
thus reflecting the very image of God.

Also procreation, another function of the family, is
linked to dominion. Why? Because it is through our children that we pass on our cultural capital of knowledge and
wealth. Both are necessary for progressive cultural development. Mankind progresses when one generation builds on
the knowledge and resources inherited from the succeeding
generation. In the Scripture, the procreation of children is
seen as a positive. They are a blessing from God.

> Lo, children are an heritage of the Lord:
>   and the fruit of the womb is his reward.
> As arrows are in the hand of a mighty man;
>   so are children of the youth.
> Happy is the man that hath his quiver full of them:
>   they shall not be ashamed,
>   but they shall speak with the enemies in the gate
>   (Psalms 127:3–5 KJV)

Or consider the entire Psalm 128:

Blessed is every one who fears the LORD,
Who walks in His ways.
When you eat the labor of your hands,
You shall be happy, and it shall be well with
    you.
Your wife shall be like a fruitful vine
In the very heart of your house,
Your children like olive plants
All around your table.
Behold, thus shall the man be blessed
Who fears the LORD.
The LORD bless you out of Zion,
And may you see the good of Jerusalem
All the days of your life.
Yes, may you see your children's children.
Peace be upon Israel!

These are just a few of the texts that show the modern notion that children are a burden who limit our freedom, or who drain our personal and social resources, is simply contrary to the Scripture and Christian tradition. While it is true that raising a family in modern America can be expensive, in many cases our reluctance to have more children is not a problem of provision but a problem of priorities. Are we willing to make the necessary sacrifices to fulfill the Cultural Mandate?

In order to fulfill the mandate it is not enough, however, simply to reproduce children. Rabbits can reproduce. We must train children. Knowledge, skill, and virtue must be transmitted from one generation to the next by the parents.

DUTIES OF CHRISTIAN PARENTS

Much of what we have to say regarding the duties of Christian parents applies to the nurture of character in general. But we will try to make our applications more directly to the area of modesty. Also, the order in which we discuss these duties is not necessarily an indication of how we rate their relative importance. Each duty is important, and each should be evident in the Christian home.

Considering our discussion of the Cultural Mandate, we'll first mention the parental duty to provide a Christian education. According to Scripture the family has an educational function. In fact, the family is, by its very nature, an educational institution; for it is in the home that children learn morality, virtue, obedience, discipline, respect, and responsibility. Thus, the primary burden for the education of children falls on the parents.

> Hear, O Israel: The LORD our God, the LORD is one!
> You shall love the LORD your God with all your
> heart, with all your soul, and with all your strength.
> "And these words which I command you today shall
> be in your heart. You shall teach them diligently
> to your children, and shall talk of them when you
> sit in your house, when you walk by the way, when
> you lie down, and when you rise up. You shall bind
> them as a sign on your hand, and they shall be as
> frontlets between your eyes. You shall write them
> on the doorposts of your house and on your gates.
> (Deuteronomy 6:4–9)

In the broadest sense of the term, *education* means the spiritual, moral, and practical development of children. They must be trained spiritually (in the Word of God), morally (in the ways of God), and practically (in the world of God). Each way is important, and all are inseparable. In the home there is really no dichotomy between spiritual or religious training and practical or vocational training. Why? Because the nature of education itself is fundamentally religious and spiritual. As one author put it, "The function of education is to school persons in the ultimate values of a culture. This is inescapably a religious task. Education has always been a religious function of society."[3] The well-known eighteenth-century theologian R. L. Dabney has made the same point: "The thing to be developed by an education is a soul, . . . among which the moral and spiritual must hold the ruling place, or else the result is a spiritual wreck and an immortal destiny ruined."[4]

Christian parents, therefore, must train their children in a biblical worldview. They should thoroughly instruct their children in the whole counsel of God, with a view to teaching them "the fear of the Lord," which is the beginning or foundation of wisdom. In Ephesians chapter 6, fathers are told how to train their children:

> Children, obey your parents in the Lord, for this is right. "Honor your father and mother," which is the first commandment with promise: "that it may be well with you and you may live long on the earth." And you, fathers, do not provoke your children to wrath, but bring them up in the training and admonition of the Lord. (Ephesians 6:1–4)

Fathers are to "bring up" their children, which means "to train by nurture" with an emphasis on gentleness and forbearance. This is opposed to "provoking" our children to anger by harshness or undue severity. Moreover, fathers are to use "training and admonition." This includes both instruction and moral warning. Taken together, these terms suggest the idea of a comprehensive education by both instruction and discipline.

It follows that Christian parents, especially the fathers, are required to provide direct instruction in the doctrines and duties of the Bible. Dad is the family theologian. He should establish a confessional home and teach his children biblical doctrines and virtues, not the least of which is modesty. One way he does this is by simple and direct teaching at home during family devotions. Modesty, as well as other Christian virtues, are clearly taught in the Bible, and it is his duty to teach his children the scheme of biblical morality. He should also teach them a broad biblical worldview, through which his children can properly interpret the world. He must teach the biblical view of the body, clothing, and sexuality. He must help them understand culture, including music and art. And he must teach them the beauty of holiness and the virtue of chastity and self-control. Dads especially need to train their sons to honor and protect femininity. Moms, likewise, must educate their daughters about femininity and sexual purity. This will include training her to exhibit modesty in her dress and demeanor.

The second duty is for Christian parents to provide a godly example. As the old adage states: "Practice is more powerful than precept." Children learn what they see exemplified in the home. If it is true that "a picture is worth a thousand words," then it is also true that "a living model is worth a million words."

The great Baptist theologian Robert Hall reminds us of the power of example:

> Nothing is more certain than that whatever we

wish others to practice, we must exemplify in our
conduct as well as enjoin. The truth of this observation extends to every branch of conduct without
exception. Would we wish to impress on young
persons a sound regard to veracity? We must maintain a strict regard to it in our own intercourse with
mankind. Are we desirous to train up our families
in the observation of the rules of justice? We must
take care to signalize our attachment to it by exemplary uprightness in our own behaviour. In every
department of moral and religious conduct, we must
not only point out the path, but lead the way. Your
wish, we take it for granted, is to train up your children in the fear of the Lord . . . Is it likely you will
succeed in that while you neglect to afford them an
example of what you wish them to practice?[5]

In order to raise godly children, we must live the
Christian life in all its fullness before their eyes so our
children may observe and imitate what we do. Yet if we
don't, our children will imitate us nonetheless. Abdica-
tion also sets a pattern they will follow. As Albert Barnes
well said:

Men do inculcate their sentiments in religion. Men
teach by example; by incidental remarks; by the
neglect of that which they regard of no value. A
man who does not pray, is teaching his children not
to pray; he who neglects the public worship of God,
is teaching his children to neglect it; he who does
not read the Bible, is teaching his children not to
read it. Such is the constitution of things, that it is
impossible for a parent not to inculcate his own religious views on his children. Since this is so, all that

the Bible requires is, that his instruction be right.[6]

Instruction is reinforced by example. A father, therefore, must model biblical virtue in its fullness. He himself must be holy and self-controlled if he would teach modesty to his children. This means the exercise of moderation in such simple things as food and drink, as well as not indulging any sexual sins of his own. Pornography of any kind is out of the question. For if Dad is defiled, his conscience will be seared and he will not be sensitive to immodesty in his own children. He must be careful in what he reads (*Sports Illustrated*), watches on television (even the commercials during football games), or sees at the movies. He must honor his wife's modesty by verbally affirming her beauty and showing her affection in front of the children. As Doug Wilson said, "A man must insist that his children honor those whom he honors, and the first one on this list should be his wife and their mother."[7]

Moms also serve as role models for their daughters in all the virtues that form the basis of modesty, whether it be self-control, decency, purity, or reverence. How she acts and dresses will be the main influence on her daughters. If she is sensual or vain, her daughters will unwittingly adopt her attitude and demeanor. Like her husband, she must not harbor any known sin, nor should she indulge in otherwise innocent activities that might foster worldliness. This may mean refraining from certain fashion magazines, talk shows, soap operas, romance novels, and movies that condone or encourage self-centeredness, vanity, or lust. "Like mother, like daughter" is a biblical proverb.

Third, parents have a duty to protect their children's purity. Instruction and example are powerful, but social forces constantly hammer away at the foundations we are attempting to lay in our children's lives. As Wells has said, postmodern instincts are formed "by the constant pounding to which we are subjected in the modern world. This pounding is made up of the pressures, demands, and expectation of our modern culture that combine to deliver the message that we must belong to it, not simply in the sense that we must live in it, but rather that we must live by it."[8]

In effect, the parents must monitor everything that their children view, read, or hear. This includes TV, movies, videos, CDs, magazines, books, and the Internet. Any of these may potentially be a channel for impurity, like a serpent, to creep into the home.

It is also necessary to know *where* your teen children are spending their time and *with whom*. The Scripture warns us repeatedly about the damaging influence of carnal friendships. For instance:

- My son, if sinners entice you, do not consent. (Proverbs 1:10)
- My son, do not walk in the way with them, Keep your foot from their path. (Proverbs 1:15)
- He that walketh with wise men shall be wise: but a companion of fools shall be destroyed. (Proverbs 13:20 KJV)
- Go from the presence of a foolish man, when you do not perceive in him the lips of knowledge. (Proverbs 14:7)
- Do not be deceived: "Evil company corrupt good habits." (1 Corinthians 15: 33)

There is really no area of your child's life that you should feel comfortable overlooking. As much as you want to assume that your child is "innocent," don't let parental affection lead to parental deception. Be on guard.

The fourth duty of parents is to perform the onerous task of discipline or punishment. This is the practical application of education and training in biblical virtue. When our children are younger this will require corporal punishment, that is, spanking; when older, other forms of discipline may be used. The mandate to discipline our children is clear and pervasive in Scripture. Just consider the following proverbs:

Proverbs 3:12—Discipline is a sign of love.

Proverbs 13:24—Discipline means love. It also must be done "early" while the child is impressionable.

Proverbs 19:18—"While there is hope" means there may be a time when it is too late. The failure to discipline because of "crying" is really a false love that leads to death.

Proverbs 22:6—Proper training will benefit the child later in life. This is a precious promise to parents.

Proverbs 22:15—Children are naturally foolish, not innately good, and thus need the "rod of correction" to drive folly far from them.

Proverbs 23:13–14—Do not withhold correction for fear of hurting the child. The rod will "deliver his soul from hell." This is why "he that spareth his rod hateth his son" (13:24 KJV).

Proverbs 29:15—The rod and reproof give wisdom. Neither is used alone; both are needed. If a child is "left to himself" (not disciplined), he will bring shame.

Proverbs 29:17—The correction of children leads to the sweet fruit of peaceful, harmonious relationships and a joyous family atmosphere. Stressful children are a sign of the parents' failure to administer biblical correction.

There are three goals of discipline. The immediate goal is prompt and cheerful obedience, while the intermediate goal is godliness or virtue. What we aim at in discipline is not a "hassle-free" life, although discipline does produce a peaceful home. No, our aim is the removal of "foolishness" from the heart and the impartation of wisdom and virtue. As our children get older, this will require us to use less punishment and more instruction. They must learn to understand the Word of God, the logic of love, and the value of virtue.

The ultimate goal of discipline, and indeed of all child training, is that our children will become not merely good, but godly. And in order for our children to become godly they need two foundational experiences: regeneration and sanctification. We must remember that our children are created in the divine image, being endowed by God with personhood. However, that image has been tarnished by the Fall. And although they retain the image of God, they have lost original righteousness. Instead of being able to exercise dominion, they are under the dominion of sin. Instead of holding communion with God, they are spiritually dead. As Doug Wilson has aptly pointed out, we must remember "that every moral monster our race has ever produced (and there have been many) was once a cute baby."[9] Cute they may be, but good they are not.

Due to both the design of creation and the effect of the Fall, your child is both splendid and sinful. Shakespeare summed up man's predicament well: "What a piece of work is man! How noble in reason! How infinite in faculty! In form, in moving, how express and admirable! In action, how like an angel! In apprehension, how like a god! The beauty of the world! The paragon of animals!" Yes, but then he goes on: "And yet, to me, what is this quintessence of dust? . . . A foul and pestilent congregation of vapors."[10]

Indeed! Both fair and fallen; both splendid and sinful. And it is this "duality" of nature that requires parents to correct and discipline sin and to lead their children to Christ. By creation the child is designed for fellowship with God; by corruption he needs to embrace Christ as Savior to be restored to God.

Thus, another duty of parents is to constantly pray for the conversion of their children. God must open the child's spiritual eyes to be regenerated. The Spirit of God must enter the child's soul, thus turning him away from darkness and sin, and toward God and holiness. The impartation of the divine life in the child's soul is really foundational to true training in virtue. But please remember that regeneration is not the same as "saying the sinner's prayer," "walking the aisle," or even being baptized. How, then, do we know if a child has been converted? The same way we know if an adult has been converted— by spiritual fruit. This would include the fruit of the Spirit (Galatians 5:22–23), love for others (1 John 3), a desire for God's Word (1 Peter 2), the practice of prayer (Matthew 6:5–13) and a spiritual understanding (1 Corinthians 3). These are just a few possible marks of conversion. If these are not present, at least in an immature expression, then it is not safe to presume that your child has been converted.

Regeneration is the beginning of new life in the soul, and the rest of the child's life should show growth in grace or progressive sanctification. The parents must constantly and earnestly pray for this growth to take place, for it is, at its deepest level, a work of God in the soul. This point can hardly be overemphasized. One of the chief problems in Christian homes today is not that the kids don't know the Bible. The real problem is that while they know the truth, they *do not love* the truth. Why? Because they are either unconverted or unsanctified. The truth of God's Word is there, so to speak, but it has no attraction to the carnal soul. Thus, Christian teens will choose to listen to vulgar music or wear scandalous clothing because their hearts, that is, their real affections, love the world and not God. The condition of the soul shapes the life—in all its choices. Simply telling your daughter that an item of clothing is inappropriate is to miss the point. The point is, *she likes it,* even though it is *morally ugly.* That's the real problem. And more rules won't fix it. What is needed is a transformation of the soul by the Word and Spirit of God. When the soul loves God, it loves holiness, which means it also loves true beauty.

What we should look for, then, is not simply a "decision," but rather a living relationship. Is my child, through the Word, prayer, and fellowship, growing in her knowledge of God and her relationship with Christ? Ultimately, we want to see that our children not only know Christ but love Him, and love Him with all their heart. Anything less is not successful Christian parenting. And anything less will not produce real modesty.

NURTURING RELATIONSHIPS

Some Christian homes are more like a boot camp, with all their rules, regulations, and schedules, than like a real home, full of love, laughter, and warm relationships. In the name of "holiness" or "godliness," the parents (usually an austere father) have pretty much made their child's life miserable by excessive legislation and severe punishment. Instead of conversations you get lectures, and instead of having a relationship you get a performance. External conformity is all-important. Follow the rules or else.

What is happening here is a substitution of moralism for true Christianity, and the result is usually rebellious children. A prime example is a woman who worked at a hair salon near our home. She was probably in her late twenties, had a butch haircut (dyed strange colors), lots of jewelry, several rings in each ear, with one ring in her tongue and another in her navel, and she wore skintight clothes with midriff and cleavage showing. She had already been married and divorced, and was now living with a boyfriend and her two kids from the first failed marriage. Judging by her appearance, you would have never guessed that this girl was raised in a "Christian home." Yet one day while talking to her we mentioned something about church and she then went on and on, telling us how her parents used to "drag me to church every Wednesday night, and twice on Sunday." She also told us that her parents had been "very strict." She even quoted a number of Bible passages for us from memory. Impressive.

So how did this poor girl from a "Christian home" end up divorced, living in sexual immorality, and dressed like a tramp? Well, after she told us her story, with quite a bit of emotional disgust toward her upbringing, we said to her: "Do you mind if we ask you a personal question?" "Go ahead," she replied. So we said, "Were you very close to your father?" Her answer didn't surprise us, though it did sadden us. "I didn't really know my father at all. He took us to church and gave us orders, but he never spent any time with us. He was always distant."

Very sad, indeed. But also very predictable. The fact is, what makes a Christian home different from a merely strict home is that a truly Christian home is built on relationships. First, a relationship with Christ, and second, relationships with one another. Within the home, the primary relationship is between husband and wife. As we learn in Ephesians 5, the marriage relationship is a living symbol of the relationship between Christ and His Bride, the church.

> Wives, submit to your own husbands, as to the Lord. For the husband is head of the wife, as also Christ is head of the church; and He is the Savior of the body. Therefore, just as the church is subject to Christ, so let the wives be to their own husbands in everything. Husbands, love your wives, just as Christ also loved the church and gave Himself for her, that He might sanctify and cleanse her with the washing of water by the word, that He might present her to Himself a glorious church, not having spot or wrinkle or any such thing, but that she should be holy and without blemish. So husbands ought to love their own wives as their own bodies; he who loves his wife loves himself. For no one ever hated his own flesh, but nourishes and cherishes it, just as the Lord does the church. For we are members of His body, of His flesh and of His bones. "For this reason a man shall leave his father and mother and be joined to his wife, and the two shall become one flesh." This is a great mystery, but I speak concerning Christ and the church. Nevertheless let each one of you in particular so love his own wife as himself, and let the wife see that she respects her

husband. (Ephesians 5:22–33)

How a Christian husband treats his wife is a statement of His view of how Christ treats His church. And how the wife responds to the husband shows the church's response to Christ. As the federal or covenantal head of the home, the husband is responsible to mirror Christ in all that he does, but especially in how he loves and nurtures his wife. His example here will shape his children's attitudes toward marriage, sexuality, and modesty. If he honors her as he should, his sons in particular will learn to honor femininity and its unique virtue, modesty. It takes a man to raise a man. And sons who are raised in a Christian home where the father loves and serves as Christ will be far less likely to encourage or condone female violations of modesty.

Moreover, the father's relationship to his child is profoundly important. For it is the father who represents God to the child. This is not to say that mothers are not important. They are. It does mean, however, that as children develop through adolescence they learn their first lessons about God from their father. As Denis Kinlaw put it: "The family is the key to getting at the right concept of God. If the family is wrong, the possibility of thinking of the true God is a problem. But if the family is right, the child—blessed by being brought up in it—is in a far stronger position to be able to grasp and make his own the deeper truths of the Christian faith." The reason, he surmises, is that "God gave us the family so that it is possible to think of him, so that all who have a father can have some basis for being able to think of the Father. And if one cannot think of God, then one is destined to live in delusion with all of its inevitable nugatory consequences."[11]

And as a godly father models his fatherhood after the heavenly Father, the child learns two fundamental realities essential to both personal and social well-being: namely, love and authority. Indeed, the child's greatest need, and the father's greatest gift, is affirmation or love. Today's crisis in "self-esteem" is really a crisis of identity resulting from the lack of paternal affection. Men and women today are insecure, neurotic, addicted, and promiscuous because they have not received proper affirmation from their fathers. Much of today's emotional and mental illness can be traced to poor or absent fathers. As Leanne Payne has noted, "Much that is called emotional illness or instability today is merely the masculine or feminine unaffirmed and out of balance within the personality."[12] This is surely one reason why we are seeing so much sexual confusion in the form of homosexuality, lesbianism, and transgenderism.

Acknowledging this fact is not a concession to pop psychology. The Bible itself calls this affirmation the "blessing."[13] There are many examples of this but perhaps the most notable is that of Christ Himself.

> Then Jesus came from Galilee to John at the Jordan to be baptized by him. And John tried to prevent Him, saying, "I need to be baptized by You, and are You coming to me?" But Jesus answered and said to him, "Permit it to be so now, for thus it is fitting for us to fulfill all righteousness." Then he allowed Him. When He had been baptized, Jesus came up immediately from the water; and behold, the heavens were opened to Him, and He saw the Spirit of God descending like a dove and alighting upon Him. And suddenly a voice came from heaven, saying, "This is My beloved Son, in whom I am well

pleased." (Matthew 3:13–17)

What we see here are the two main aspects of the blessing: physical touch and spoken affirmation. The Spirit of God in the form of a dove descended upon and touched Jesus, even as His Father spoke the words of affirmation: "This is My beloved Son, in whom I am well pleased." And it is no coincidence that this blessing took place as a prelude to Christ's entering the wilderness to be tested. For it was Christ's *very identity* as the Son of God that was tested there: "*If* you are the son of God . . ." Being fortified by His Father's love, Christ was able to resist the temptation to deny His own identity as Messiah.

Moreover, children also learn from their fathers to respect authority. Although in a Christian home both parents have genuine authority, the father is the locus of that authority. And if children do not learn to respect parental authority, then their respect for all other authorities is weakened, leading to increasing social disintegration. As the late R. J. Rushdoony put it:

> Without the authority of the family, a society
> quickly moves into social anarchy. The source of
> the family's authority is God; the immediate locale
> of the authority is the father or husband (1 Corin-
> thians 11:1–15). The abdication by the father of his
> authority, or the denial of his authority, leads to the
> social anarchy described by Isaiah (3:12). Women
> rule over men; children then gain undue freedom
> and power and become oppressors of their parents;
> the emasculated rulers in such a social order lead
> the people astray and destroy the fabric of society.
> The end result is social collapse and captivity (Isa-

iah 3:16–26), and a situation of danger and ruin for women, a time of "reproach" or "disgrace," in which the once independent and feministic women are humbled in their pride and seek the protection and safety of a man. . . . Isaiah clearly saw the absence of the man's authority as productive of social chaos.[14]

As it turns out, modern social research has confirmed Isaiah's vision. Children from fatherless homes are much more likely to do poorly in school and to turn to violence and crime. This is especially true of boys. "In social terms, the primary results of decultured paternity are a decline in children's well-being and a rise in male violence, especially against women."[15] Sadly, this is one reason we are witnessing such a staggering increase in stalking, harassment, and date rape.[16] And it is also a reason we have so much pornography; for pornography is simply another form of violence toward women.

What, then, is the link to modesty? It is this: By blending both love and authority, a godly father provides his child proper self-esteem and also respect for others. A daughter who feels truly loved by her father will not need to disrobe for male attention. In fact, she will have too much self-respect to be shameless. Wendy Shalit proudly stated: "I'm a much stronger person for having a 'paternalistic' father who is always telling me what to do. I know he's that way because he loves me."[17]

She also tells the story of psychologist Mary Pipher, who just doesn't understand "Jody," a girl from a conservative and paternalistic home. In contrast to the many girls who have eating disorders or who are mutilating themselves, Pipher doesn't understand why "a girl raised in such an authoritarian . . . family" should be "so well liked, outgoing and self-confident." "Why did she have less anger and more respect for adults?" "Why was she so relaxed when many girls are so angst-filled and angry?"[18] The answer is that she had a good relationship with her dad—a strong but loving father.

Moreover, our young men will be taught to honor others. As they are taught to honor virtue and modesty, they will also honor and respect woman and not view them as sexual objects to be used, abused, and discarded. Thus, not only will our young teenage girls be strong enough in their identity to resist the social pressures to conform to worldly types of dress or behavior, but our young men will not be inducing our girls to be immodest.

Most important, the child's relationship to the father is the bridge for truth to travel from the father's heart to the child's. All that we have said about the parents' and father's role in instruction really hinges on his having a personal relationship with his child. If he would teach his child virtue, then he must make his instruction palatable by being personal. The child, instead of seeing the father as a distant tyrant who wants to control his life, will see the father as a sacrificial shepherd who lays down his life for the sheep. It is easy to bow to a blood-dipped rod.

10

In the Courts of the Lord

If a woman, when going to public worship, looks in the glass, and contemplates, with a secret self-complacence, the figure which it reflects to her view, I am afraid she is not in the frame of spirit most suitable for one, who is about to cry for mercy as a miserable sinner.

JOHN NEWTON

IN HIS FIRST LETTER TO Timothy, the apostle Paul lays down guidelines to govern the Christian community or church. Though first given to the church at Ephesus, the principles enunciated here are applicable to the church in all ages. Paul's concern here is "church order"—how men and women of faith are to conduct themselves in the "church of the living God, the pillar and ground of the truth" (3:15). Men (literally, *the* men) are exhorted to "pray everywhere without wrath and doubting," while the women are told to "adorn themselves in modest apparel and good works."

This text in particular teaches us that God cares not only how we "do church," but, more specifically, He cares how women behave and dress "in church." Therefore, modesty is a "church issue." The church, like the family, has a role in forming the character of its members, and seeing that the female followers of Christ develop the virtue of modesty. What, then, must the church do to cultivate virtue?

PROCLAMATION OF THE WORD

The place to begin is in the Word. For every reformation in the history of the church has been associated with the teaching and proclamation of the Scripture. The words of Robert Candlish, a nineteenth-century minister of Scotland, put the matter squarely before us:

> The word of God then is the instrument in every truly religious movement, whether on a large or on a limited scale. It is the truth contained in that word which alone can savingly enlighten and impress either individual minds in slow succession, or an entire congregation or community together. In every work of the Holy Spirit this instrumentality is employed, and the work is genuine and trustworthy only in so far as it is a legitimate effect of this cause. Various agencies may be adopted in order to bring the word of God to bear on the souls of those whom it is intended to move. It may be directly taught and enforced by reading and expounding, by preaching, by conference and meditation, by the catechizing of the young, by pressing it, in short, in every form of persuasion and of warning, on the hearts and consciences of all. Its truth may be symbolically represented, sealed and applied, by sacramental emblems. It may be indirectly commended and carried home by circumstances fitted to give weight and beauty to its lessons, as by providential visitations, by the example of those who adorn its doctrine, or by the sympathy of a general spiritual awakening. Still in

every case, if the effect produced is really divine,
divine truth must be the immediate cause; and the
word is that truth.[1]

All of the Word is important, and all of it should
be proclaimed from our pulpits. However, the modern
church in particular needs a restored vision of God Himself, because a proper view of God is the greatest need of
both the individual Christian and the corporate church.
As A. W. Tozer rightly said: "The low view of God enter-
tained almost universally among Christians is the cause
of a hundred lesser evils everywhere among us. . . . It is
impossible to keep our moral practices sound and our
inward attitudes right while our idea of God is erroneous or inadequate."[2] Could there be a connection, then,
between our low view of God and the cultural captivity of
the church? Indeed, there is. David Wells, in reporting on
the state of the modern American pulpit, put his finger on
the root issue. We are ignoring God Himself.

> Even more significant than these findings was a
> discovery relating to the orientation of the sermons.
> Only 19.5 percent were grounded in or related in
> any way to the nature, character, and will of God.
> At issue here is not whether the sermons were *about*
> God; there are many other legitimate subjects about
> which a preacher might wish to discourse on a Sun-
> day morning. Rather, at issue is whether the real-
> ity, character, and acts of God provided an explicit
> foundation for what the preacher said about the life
> of faith, or whether the life of faith was presented as
> making some kind of internal sense without refer-
> ence to the character, will, and acts of God. At issue,
> in short, was the prevailing Geist in today's pulpit.

Is it anthropocentric or is it theocentric? The overwhelming proportion of sermons analyzed—more than 80 percent—were anthropocentric. It is as if God has become an awkward appendage to the practice of evangelical faith, at least as measured by the pulpit. Indeed, it would seem from these sermons that God and the supernatural order are related only with difficulty to the life of faith; in any event, He does not seem to be at its center. Contemporary sermons are reserving the center for the issues that engage us in the course of life, or, more specifically, for the self. It is around this surrogate center that God and his world are made to spin.[3]

It's not that we have denied God. We just don't pay much attention to Him. He's like the elderly grandpa we put in the nursing home. We know He's there, and we really do care about Him (at least in our hearts); it's just that we only visit Him a couple of times a year. This won't do, of course, because what we believe about God will shape every area of our lives. "Actual behavior infallibly betrays the real object of a man's worship."[4]

If we really care about restoring virtue in the church, then we must first restore God to His rightful place as the center of all that we do both privately and corporately. A peripheral God will change nothing. This means that we uphold and declare His Word as the standard of our faith and practice—in every area of life. We teach and preach the whole counsel of God and not just those doctrines that lie cozily on the conscience of modernity. We must preach God's attributes, God's will, God's law, God's kingdom, God's church, God's plan—indeed, we must preach Him back into the center of our lives. Only then will lives change. We must come to understand that our problem isn't dysfunction. It's sin. We have offended a holy God. We need the atonement that only He provides. Our quest for happiness in the fool's paradise of pornography is not just futile; it provokes the anger of God, for He is a jealous God. We must repent, therefore, not only of our sin, but of perhaps the greatest sin of all: trivializing Him, which is idolatry. There is no other word for it.

When the Lord takes His throne in the church once again, we can then begin to teach our people the meaning of holiness. For He is its source and embodiment. Again and again we are told in His Word: "Be ye holy for I the Lord am holy." We must repudiate the notion of cheap grace as we allow the brightness of God's holiness to shine on the darkness of our lives. We must not only see our sin; we must see it as He sees. For only then will we truly abhor it and strive to be holy. And in teaching holiness we will be restoring modesty, for holiness is its soil.

THE CENTRALITY OF WORSHIP

In addition, the restoration of God will surely lead to a restoration of worship. The grand object or purpose of the church is to glorify God through worship. It's "grand" not only because God Himself is grand, but also because worship, in the broadest sense of the word, is the comprehensive goal of all that we do. We desire to honor and glorify God in all things. This theme of worship comes out very strongly in Revelation:

> Before the throne there was a sea of glass, like crystal. And in the midst of the throne, and around the throne, were four living creatures full of eyes in

front and in back. The first living creature was like a lion, the second living creature like a calf, the third living creature had a face like a man, and the fourth living creature was like a flying eagle. The four living creatures, each having six wings, were full of eyes around and within. And they do not rest day or night, saying:

"Holy, holy, holy,
Lord God Almighty,
Who was and is and is to come!"

Whenever the living creatures give glory and honor and thanks to Him who sits on the throne, who lives forever and ever, the twenty-four elders fall down before Him who sits on the throne and worship Him who lives forever and ever, and cast their crowns before the throne, saying:

"You are worthy, O Lord,
To receive glory and honor and power;
For You created all things,
And by Your will they exist and were created." (Revelation 4:6–1)

After these things I looked, and behold, a great multitude which no one could number, of all nations, tribes, peoples, and tongues, standing before the throne and before the Lamb, clothed with white robes, with palm branches in their hands, and crying out with a loud voice, saying, "Salvation belongs to our God who sits on the throne, and to the Lamb!" All the angels stood around the throne and the elders and the four living creatures, and fell on their faces before the throne and worshiped God, saying:

"Amen! Blessing and glory and wisdom,
Thanksgiving and honor and power and

might,
Be to our God forever and ever. Amen."
Then one of the elders answered, saying to me,
"Who are these arrayed in white robes, and where
did they come from?" (Revelation 7:9–17)

It is clear from these passages (not to mention many others) that biblical worship is theocentric and Christocentric. Put simply, the focus of worship is the Godhead. God, not man, is center stage. So, when we gather for worship, our full attention ought to be on the Lord, and we should do nothing that would detract from that focus. In fact, Paul's admonition to women in 1 Timothy 2:9 is given in the context of corporate worship. The men are to lift up holy hands in prayer. The women should do likewise, but with the additional directive to regulate their demeanor and dress with modesty. As A. C. Hervey put it:

> Christians come to church to worship a glorious
> God, to humble themselves before his holy presence, and to hear his Word, not for display, not to
> attract notice, not for vain-glory or worldly vanity.
> It is, therefore, quite out of place for either men or
> women to make a parade of finery in church. The
> ornaments best suited for persons professing godliness at all times, but especially when they approach
> the throne of God, are those of a pure heart and a
> meek spirit, and an abundance of good works. It is
> the hidden man of the heart which needs adorning
> for its access to the court of heaven.[5]

Yet, a person who attends church dressed immodestly is specifically trying to get attention. Thus, an immodest worshiper is an oxymoron—a contradiction in terms.

But worse, an immodest worshiper is a hindrance to those who are striving to fully focus on Christ. It is a frightening thought, but if a woman comes to church dressed to get attention, then she is competing with Christ.

A second observation about these heavenly worship scenes: the texts make a point of stating what the worshipers were wearing. They were dressed in white robes. It is striking that, with the main point of the text being the honor and praise of God, apparel is even mentioned at all. Thus, it must be important, and indeed it is. For the white robes signify both purity (white) and modesty (robes). And our worship should be the same—pure and modest. All throughout Scripture the proper response to God's presence is to cover up. Even the seraphim, who dwell in God's presence, use their wings to cover their bodies (Isaiah 6:2; Ezekiel 1:11).

In addition, we see in these and other passages that corporate worship is not just something we do in our hearts. While worship should be done from the heart, it is expressed through our bodies. As noted earlier, our bodies are temples of the Holy Spirit, and we, as God's chosen people, are ordained to offer the spiritual sacrifice of praise, which is the fruit of our lips. Though we worship God in spirit and in truth, we also worship Him with our bodily members. The great Puritan theologian Stephen Charnock argued this convincingly in his classic work on the attribute of God. He said, "As God under the ceremonial law did not command the worship of the body and the observation of outward rites without the engagement of the spirit, so neither doth he command that of the spirit without the peculiar attendance of the body. . . . Our bodies as well as our spirits are to be presented to God. Our bodies in lieu of the sacrifices of beasts, as in the Judaical institutions; body for the whole man; a living sacrifice, not to be slain, as the beasts were, but living a new life, in a holy posture, with crucified affections."[6]

COMMUNITY AND LIBERTY

By its very nature, the church is a community. Jesus said, "Where *two or three* are gathered in My name, I am there in the midst of them" (Matthew 18:20). In order to have the church present, there must be a plurality of persons. Thus, although the church is one, the church is also many. For instance, the apostle Paul told the Corinthians, "For as the body is one and has many members, but all the members of that one body, being many, are one body, so also is Christ" (1 Corinthians 12:12). And to the Ephesians he said: "There is one body and one Spirit, just as you were called in one hope of your calling; one Lord, one faith, one baptism; one God and Father of all, who is above all, and through all, and in you all" (Ephesians 4:4–6).

This unity of the body of Christ relates to modesty because our membership in the church lays upon us certain duties inherent in community life. Living in community means our lives are not our own. We are required to be conscious of how our lives, including our speech, conduct, and dress, impact those around us. Fellowship, or "body life," as it is called, carries the responsibilities of mutual respect and mutual accountability. In a word, our liberty is limited by community.

As it pertains to modesty, out of respect for others, we should not dress or behave in a way that causes offense to others in our community. We avoid immodesty not simply because it is sinful in itself, but because as Christians living in community, how we dress and behave impacts others. Clothing, by its very nature, is for public consumption, and we must not dress in a way that causes others to stumble, offends them, or leads them to sinful thoughts. Modest attire will avoid the extremes of ostentatious display, sensual allurement, confused androgyny, and sinful association.

Writing to the Corinthians about eating meat offered to idols, a practice that was offending some, Paul said:

> Now concerning things offered to idols: We know
> that we all have knowledge. Knowledge puffs
> up, but love edifies. And if anyone thinks that
> he knows anything, he knows nothing yet as he
> ought to know. But if anyone loves God, this one
> is known by Him. Therefore concerning the eat-
> ing of things offered to idols, we know that an idol
> is nothing in the world, and that there is no other
> God but one. For even if there are so-called gods,
> whether in heaven or on earth (as there are many
> gods and many lords), yet for us there is one God,
> the Father, of whom are all things, and we for Him;
> and one Lord Jesus Christ, through whom are all
> things, and through whom we live. However, there
> is not in everyone that knowledge; for some, with
> consciousness of the idol, until now eat it as a thing
> offered to an idol; and their conscience, being weak,
> is defiled. But food does not commend us to God;
> for neither if we eat are we the better, nor if we do
> not eat are we the worse. But beware lest somehow
> this liberty of yours become a stumbling block to
> those who are weak. For if anyone sees you who
> have knowledge eating in an idol's temple, will not

the conscience of him who is weak be emboldened
to eat those things offered to idols? And because of
your knowledge shall the weak brother perish, for
whom Christ died? But when you thus sin against
the brethren, and wound their weak conscience,
you sin against Christ. Therefore, if food makes my
brother stumble, I will never again eat meat, lest I
make my brother stumble. (1 Corinthians 8:1–13)

Later on, in chapter 10, Paul says:

But if anyone says to you, "This was offered to
idols," do not eat it for the sake of the one who told
you, and for conscience' sake; for "the earth is the
Lord's, and all its fullness." "Conscience," I say,
not your own, but that of the other. For why is my
liberty judged by another man's conscience? But
if I partake with thanks, why am I evil spoken of
for the food over which I give thanks? Therefore,
whether you eat or drink, or whatever you do, do all
to the glory of God. Give no offense, either to the
Jews or to the Greeks or to the church of God, just
as I also please all men in all things, not seeking my
own profit, but the profit of many, that they may be
saved. (1 Corinthians 10:28–33)

The church in Rome was having related problems
with disputes about food, fasts, and feast days. Paul gave
them similar advice. "Therefore let us not judge one
another anymore, but rather resolve this, not to put a
stumbling block or a cause to fall in our brother's way"
(Romans 14:13). "Therefore let us pursue the things
which make for peace and the things by which one may
edify another" (Romans 14:19). Concluding his comments

to the Romans on this subject Paul said: "We then who are strong ought to bear with the scruples of the weak, and not to please ourselves. Let each of us please his neighbor for his good, leading to edification. For even Christ did not please Himself; but as it is written, 'The reproaches of those who reproached You fell on Me'" (Romans 15:1–3).

Now, the parallel to modesty is plain. Clothing is a "nonessential" issue, that is, it is not essential to salvation. And, at the same time, there are differing views that are causing conflict within the church. So, what we learn from Paul is that there really is such a thing as Christian liberty in things indifferent (*adiaphora*). And clothing styles would certainly qualify as one of those things. Even though we may have every right to indulge a certain practice or to wear a certain type of clothing, it does not necessarily follow that it is best to do so.

What is to guide our decision? First, even though our liberty is real, our liberty is never to be used for selfish ends or to hurt others. On the contrary, liberty is to be used for the benefit and edification of the church. The simple fact is, when a Christian woman dresses in a provocative way, she is hurting her brothers in Christ. Men, by their very design, are prone to lust, which takes years of discipline and growth to conquer. An immodest woman is a provocation to sin for a man. She is (knowingly or not) enticing him to lust, and should he give in, she has burdened his conscience. As Pollard has said:

> Women should be especially aware of how their
> clothing impacts men; because generally speaking,
> men are far more visually oriented than women.
> Richard Baxter wisely commented that women sin

when their clothing tends "to the ensnaring of the
minds of the beholders in shameless, lustful, wanton
passions, though you say, you intend it not, it is your
sin, that you do that which probably will procure
it, yea, that you did to your best to avoid it. And
though it be their sin and vanity that is the cause,
it is nevertheless your sin to be the unnecessary
occasion: for you must consider that you live among
diseased souls! And you must not lay a stumbling-
block in their way, nor blow up the fire of their lust,
nor make your ornaments their snares; but must
walk among sinful persons, as you would do with a
candle among straw or gunpowder; or else you may
see the flame which you would not foresee, when it
is too late to quench it."[7]

Of course, she can say she has the "liberty" to dress
as she pleases, and that "he's the one with the problem,"
not her. True enough. In fact, that's the very point we
are making: men do have a problem with lust; therefore,
Christian women should not do anything to inflame that
lust. As Paul said, we should not use our liberty if it harms
others. And immodesty harms both men and women.

Second, the overarching purpose of the Christian life,
which is serving Christ and glorifying God, should also
govern the use of our liberty. Everything the believer does
should be designed to bring glory to God. Do we thus glorify God when we draw attention to ourselves by our dress,
or cause others to sin by our appearance?

Third, the grand rule of Christian fellowship is love.
"Yet if your brother is grieved because of your food, you
are no longer walking in love" (Romans 14:15). The same
is true of clothes. If your brother is grieved by your cloth-

ing, and yet you insist on dressing that way, then you have demonstrated that you do not love your brother. You really love yourself. What is more important, your hot clothes or his holy conscience?

And fourth, those who are strong, that is, those who understand their liberty, must be willing to sacrifice their liberty for the benefit of the weak. This is the logical corollary of true brotherly love, for love by its very nature is sacrificial. In situations of conflict and difference of opinion, the burden to sacrifice falls on the strong, or those who are more knowledgeable and mature. Indeed, the failure to sacrifice one's liberty for the benefit of a brother in Christ not only demonstrates a lack of love, it likewise reveals spiritual immaturity. A woman who is truly godly should be willing to forgo any attire or behavior that is a source of pain to other Christians. And her failure to do so simply shows that she is not really godly. Though she "professes godliness," she is not acting according to its principles.

Community also entails mutual accountability. Because our clothing is for public consumption, and because it does influence other people, we must take responsibility for its effect. But this also requires the willingness to be held accountable for one's influence on that community. In other words, each of us should be willing to hear words of correction or admonition from others, even regarding our clothing. A question every woman ought to ask herself is this: If my attire were causing my brothers in Christ to sin, would I want to know? Her answer is a good barometer of her spirituality.

But would anyone dare to tell her? Sadly, in many churches the answer is no. For all too often our churches are inhabited by strangers who congregate once a week for an hourly lecture. But in a church patterned after the New Testament model of genuine fellowship, relationships should be deep and strong, where members care enough to "[speak] the truth in love" (Ephesians 4:15) and "consider one another in order to stir up love and good works" (Hebrews 10:24). We edify the body of Christ by instruction, admonition, and reproof. In a word, we care enough to confront. Thus, the church must mature to the point that, as a community, we are willing to both exhort and reprove others, and to receive the same from others. And this mutual admonition and accountability apply to all sorts of things, including modesty.

The pulpit ministry of the church must begin to teach on the subject of modesty. Until that happens, not only will the problem continue to grow, but the average member will not feel free to hold others accountable. The leadership of the church, therefore, needs to make modesty a topic of discussion and study. And after properly instructing the church on biblical standards, the leadership must be willing to speak in love to anyone who continues to "strut their stuff."

We would add that one of the most powerful forms of instruction is example. Therefore, the leadership of any church must evaluate its own example in the area of modesty. Men and women on a church staff must realize that they are an example in every area of their lives. This includes how they dress. If the deacons come to church in blue jeans, you can be sure that the members will be comfortable doing the same. If the pastors' or deacons' wives are dressed attractively yet modestly, then they will set a powerful example for the rest of the women in the church. For the most part, the "culture" of a local church will reflect the priorities and patterns set by the teaching and example of the leadership. The virtues of the leaders become those of the church.

SACRAMENT AND SANCTIFICATION

Another important goal of the church is sanctification. One way this is accomplished is through the sacraments, or what are called the "means of grace"—Baptism and Communion (the Lord's Supper). Each sacrament is a physical sign or incarnational symbol. In baptism the sign is the water; in Communion the sign is the bread and wine. These signs signify important truths about our salvation. The point to make here is that the signs are *physical* and that each sacrament applies to the *body*. In baptism our bodies are washed; in Communion we take Christ's body into our bodies. At a minimum, the sacraments teach us the importance of dedicating our bodies to God for His glory. Specifically, the sacraments speak of the cleansing of both soul and body that is accomplished by Christ's work.

And this leads us to mention that sanctification, which literally means to be "set apart," is both positional and practical. Positionally, the believer is already set apart for God, and that is why all Christians are called "saints" in Scripture. "Saint" and "sanctification" and "holy" all come from the same root word. God has chosen us and set us apart for Himself. Yet, what is true positionally ought to be true practically. We ought to be set apart from sin and evil. And this practical or experiential sanctification applies not only to the soul, but also to the body. As Paul told the Corinthians,

Do not be unequally yoked together with unbeliev-
ers. For what fellowship has righteousness with
lawlessness? And what communion has light with
darkness? And what accord has Christ with Belial?
Or what part has a believer with an unbeliever?
And what agreement has the temple of God with
idols? For you are the temple of the living God. As
God has said:

> "I will dwell in them
> And walk among them.
> I will be their God,
> And they shall be My people."

Therefore

> "Come out from among them
> And be separate, says the Lord.
> Do not touch what is unclean,
> And I will receive you."
> "I will be a Father to you,
> And you shall be My sons and daughters,
> Says the LORD Almighty."

Therefore, having these promises, beloved, let us
cleanse ourselves from all filthiness of the flesh and
spirit, perfecting holiness in the fear of God.
(2 Corinthians 6:14–7:1)

God has called the church to be a holy people, a holy
community of worshipers who are set apart from moral
evil, and who worship God in the beauty of holiness. It
is a holy God who walks in our midst. We must be holy
for Him. And our holiness will be reflected in how we
worship, how we pray, how we serve, and even in how we
dress. In the presence of the Holy, we cover ourselves.

The Beauty of Modesty

11

Present Your Bodies

If you would be a good Christian, there is but one way, you must live wholly unto God; and if you would live wholly unto God, you must live according to the wisdom that comes from God; you must act according to right judgments of the nature and value of things; you must live in the exercise of holy and heavenly affections and use all the gifts of God to His praise and glory.

WILLIAM LAW

IS IT POSSIBLE FOR TODAY'S Christian woman to live a life of modesty? Can she maintain a virtuous walk in a vulgar world? We believe that she can. But it will take a deep and serious commitment, for nearly everything in our culture is trying to seduce her to compromise—to be cool, to be sexy, to be hip, to be hot. The world is trying to mold her into its erotic image, to make her sexy, not spiritual. And to resist this pressure requires total consecration. Halfhearted soldiers don't win military wars. And halfhearted Christians don't win spiritual wars.

A CALL TO CONSECRATION

In Romans 12:1–2 the apostle Paul calls all Christians to a life of consecration:

> I beseech you therefore, brethren, by the mercies of
> God, that you present your bodies a living sacrifice,

holy, acceptable to God, which is your reasonable
service. And do not be conformed to this world, but
be transformed by the renewing of your mind, that
you may prove what is that good and acceptable and
perfect will of God.

This is a call to full and absolute surrender to the will
of God. We are to present "our bodies," that is, our entire
selves, to God in order to live in a manner that is pleasing to Him. Using the imagery of the Old Testament sacrifices, we are bid to come and lay ourselves on God's altar
and there to die to the world and to self. But we don't just
die; we are to be "living sacrifices," which means we are to
live totally dedicated to God. This is no halfway measure.
The animal sacrifices were not wounded; they were killed.
And if we wish to please God with our lives, we must
determine to fully surrender all to Him. But what God is
really after is our hearts, for if He has that, He has all that
we are. If we are His, then our bodies are His. And if our
bodies are His, then our clothes are His.

This call to full consecration, says Paul, is our "reasonable service." In light of what God has done for us
in Christ—in light of Christ's death to save us from the
judgment of God; in light of God's free pardon of our
sins by grace; in light of our reconciliation, justification, redemption, and even our future glorification—it
is surely "reasonable" to respond with giving our all to
Him. Didn't He do the same for us when He gave us
Christ? In response to God's great love for us, we love
Him in return.

THE GREAT COMMANDMENT

According to Jesus, love for God is the first, or greatest, commandment.

> You shall love the LORD your God with all your
> heart, with all your soul, and with all your mind.
> This is the first and great commandment. (Matthew
> 22:37–38)

Nothing, absolutely nothing, is more important than this. It is, or should be, our first priority, our utmost concern. For if we are wrong here, we are building our lives on a shaky foundation; but if we are right here, we are building on the Rock. God is concerned not only with the outward actions and attire but also with the desires of the heart.

What, then, does it mean to love God first? One of the best descriptions is given by Adam Clarke:

> Hence, it appears that, by this love, the soul eagerly
> cleaves to, affectionately admires, and constantly
> rests in God, supremely pleased and satisfied with
> him as its portion: that it acts from him, as its
> author; for him, as its master; and to him, as its
> end. That, by it, all the powers and faculties of the
> mind are concentrated in the Lord of the universe.
> That, by it, the whole man is willingly surrendered
> to the Most High: and that, through it, an identity,
> or sameness of spirit with the Lord is acquired—the
> man being made a partaker of the divine nature,
> having the mind in him which was in Christ, and
> thus dwelling in God, and God in him.[1]

It is vital to see that Jesus does not just call us to "love God." He adds the all important words, "with *all* your heart, *all* your soul, *all* your mind, and *all* your strength."

That simple word, *all*, captures the essence of real Christianity. Consider the comments of Albert Barnes:

> [Thou shalt love the Lord thy God with all thy heart.] The meaning of this is, thou shalt love him with all thy faculties or powers. Thou shalt love him supremely, more than all other beings and things, and with all the ardor possible. To love him with all the heart is to fix the affections supremely on him, more strongly than on anything else, and to be willing to give up all that we hold dear at his command.
>
> [With all thy soul] Or, with all thy "life." This means, to be willing to give up the life to him, and to devote it all to his service; to live to him, and to be willing to die at his command.
>
> [With all thy mind] To submit the "intellect" to his will. To love his law and gospel more than we do the decisions of our own minds. To be willing to submit all our faculties to his teaching and guidance, and to devote to him all our intellectual attainments and all the results of our intellectual efforts.
>
> [With all thy strength] With all the faculties of soul and body. To labor and toil for his glory, and to make that the great object of all our efforts.[2]

Thus, we are not to love the Lord as one love among many, but we are to love Him first and foremost—supremely. And we are to love Him with ardor, conviction, earnestness, and passion—fervently.

The Christian woman who loves God first loves Him and His will more than she loves fashion or jewelry or clothes. She loves Him more than the applause of the world or the praise of men. Like the apostle Paul, she will gladly count all things loss to gain the excellency of the knowledge of Christ. Like David, she will desire to "behold the beauty of the Lord." And like Mary, she will choose the one thing necessary, communing with Christ. In loving God, she will be more heavenly minded than earthly minded. She will be more concerned to cultivate her soul than to captivate spectators. She will renounce the world to follow her Lord.

A Life of Discipleship

On one occasion we were invited to minister to the youth of a Midwestern church. While there, we met a native pastor from a third-world country. In our conversation he made this telling observation: "In America, you ask the question 'When did you become a Christian?' But in my country people ask, 'When did you repent?'"

Indeed, much that is wrong with the church is partly a result of misunderstanding the real nature of the Christian life. While we say that a Christian is someone who "accepts Christ into his heart," or one who "believes in Jesus as Savior," it is striking how seldom such phraseology occurs in the Bible itself. In fact, the characteristic word in the New Testament for a believer in Christ is not "Christian," but the Greek word *mathetes*, which means "disciple." It is used 260 times in the Gospels and Acts alone. So, whereas we say, "I am a Christian," they would have said, "I am a disciple of Christ." The difference is momentous. If a Christian woman wants to cultivate the virtue of modesty, then she must be more than a nominal believer. She must be a true disciple.

What does this mean? First, a true disciple of Christ is a learner or student. As Christ himself said, to be a disciple means to learn specifically of Him.

At that time Jesus answered and said, "I thank You,
Father, Lord of heaven and earth, that You have
hidden these things from the wise and prudent and
have revealed them to babes. Even so, Father, for so
it seemed good in Your sight. All things have been
delivered to Me by My Father, and no one knows
the Son except the Father. Nor does anyone know
the Father except the Son, and the one to whom
the Son wills to reveal Him. Come to Me, all you
who labor and are heavy laden, and I will give you
rest. Take My yoke upon you and learn from Me, for
I am gentle and lowly in heart, and you will find rest
for your souls. For My yoke is easy and My burden is
light." (Matthew 11:25–30)

As one author put it: "Greek pupils and rabbini-
cal students bound themselves personally to their master
and looked for objective teaching, with the ultimate aim
of themselves becoming a master or rabbi."[3] Whereas the
first disciples were able to sit at Jesus's feet—physically—
we, on the other hand, must learn of Jesus through both
His Word and His Spirit. Thus, we must be serious students of the Scriptures. We must read, meditate upon, and
study them. Since Christ is the *Logos*, or revealer of God,
all the Scripture is from Him, and we must be students of
the whole Bible. An ignorant disciple is an oxymoron.

Of course, any woman who has known Christ for any
length of time knows that she is supposed to read her Bible
or have what is called a "quiet time." So perhaps it seems
we are belaboring the obvious. Yet the sad fact today is
that there is widespread biblical illiteracy in our Evangelical churches. For instance, one survey of "Christians"
yielded these sad results:

- 49 percent polled said that Satan was not a living entity but only a symbol of evil.
- 39 percent said if a person is "good," they will earn a place in heaven.
- 29 percent said that when Jesus was on earth He committed sins like other people.[4]

Other surveys show similarly dismal figures.

Now, in charity we hope these people may indeed be Christians; that is, we hope they have truly embraced Christ as Savior. But they are not disciples in the biblical sense of the term; for a true disciple is a student of God's Word and knows the truth. Any woman who wants to be a disciple of Christ will study what His Word says about the virtue of modesty. And upon learning His will, she will take His yoke upon her.

Second, a disciple is an imitator. When calling the original disciples, Jesus said: "*Follow* Me, and I will make you fishers of men." To "follow" means to imitate, to pattern our lives on the life of Christ. Thus, first we learn of Jesus, and then, based upon that knowledge, we imitate Jesus. We believe what He believed and live as He lived. As it relates to modesty, Jesus certainly possessed the spiritual qualities of decency, self-control, chastity, and reverence. Indeed, we could say He was, and is, the ultimate example of all virtue. For He was the only man who ever lived a sinless human life. He never had an impure thought or suggested one by His dress or demeanor. Holiness was His garment.

Third, a disciple is one who abides with the Master. As Verbrugge rightly notes, the term *mathetes* "indicates discipleship as total attachment to someone, not [merely] the Greek idea of pupil."[5] In order to be a disciple, we must abide. This means that we practice the fine art of personal communion with Christ. To abide with Him means to know Him in a very personal, vital, and continual way. According to Jesus:

> I am the true vine, and My Father is the vine-
> dresser. Every branch in Me that does not bear
> fruit He takes away; and every branch that bears
> fruit He prunes, that it may bear more fruit. You
> are already clean because of the word which I have
> spoken to you. Abide in Me, and I in you. As the
> branch cannot bear fruit of itself, unless it abides in
> the vine, neither can you, unless you abide in Me.
> I am the vine, you are the branches. He who abides
> in Me, and I in him, bears much fruit; for without
> Me you can do nothing. If anyone does not abide in
> Me, he is cast out as a branch and is withered; and
> they gather them and throw them into the fire, and
> they are burned. If you abide in Me, and My words
> abide in you, you will ask what you desire, and it
> shall be done for you. By this My Father is glori-
> fied, that you bear much fruit; so you will be My
> disciples. As the Father loved Me, I also have loved
> you; abide in My love. If you keep My command-
> ments, you will abide in My love, just as I have
> kept My Father's commandments and abide in His
> love. These things I have spoken to you, that My
> joy may remain in you, and that your joy may be
> full. (John 15:1–11)

In practice, abiding means private devotions, such as meditation and prayer, as well as public devotions, worship, and instruction. In sum, we might say that "abiding" means learning to walk with Jesus on a daily basis. It is in this daily communion with Christ that real transformation of character takes place. Without this, the Christian life will be an empty shell. With it, there will be a gradual but radical makeover of the mind, an overhaul of the heart, and a renovation of the affections. Slowly but surely, the very image and virtue of Jesus Christ will be formed in the soul. The character of Christ becomes manifest in the character of the disciple.

Without this, all external alterations are in vain. A woman may comply with external changes in her wardrobe, but if her heart is not near to Christ, those changes are merely cosmetic and probably won't last very long. What Christ wants is not a mere change of clothes. He is looking for a change of heart, a change of mind, a change of life. And the desire and power for that change comes only from daily communion with Jesus Himself. This is no mere cliché. We cannot attain virtue apart from Christ. So great is the damage to our nature from the Fall that nothing can repair the ruins but the Creator Himself. Abiding in Him, communion works restoration.

And fourth, a disciple is one who obeys. All that we have said suggests obedience. Surely if we learn of Christ's will but do not do it, then we are not living as a disciple. In fact, in the Scripture, "the goal of learning is action that corresponds to God's Word."[6] In other words, speculative knowledge alone is never the goal of Christian instruction. As the apostle James put it:

> Therefore lay aside all filthiness and overflow
> of wickedness, and receive with meekness the
> implanted word, which is able to save your souls.
> But be doers of the word, and not hearers only,

deceiving yourselves. For if anyone is a hearer of the word and not a doer, he is like a man observing his natural face in a mirror; for he observes himself, goes away, and immediately forgets what kind of man he was. But he who looks into the perfect law of liberty and continues in it, and is not a forgetful hearer but a doer of the work, this one will be blessed in what he does. (James 1:21–25)

Our Lord Himself said that the way to know a real disciple is to look at the fruit.

Beware of false prophets, who come to you in sheep's clothing, but inwardly they are ravenous wolves. You will know them by their fruits. Do men gather grapes from thorn-bushes or figs from thistles? Even so, every good tree bears good fruit, but a bad tree bears bad fruit. A good tree cannot bear bad fruit, nor can a bad tree bear good fruit. Every tree that does not bear good fruit is cut down and thrown into the fire. Therefore by their fruits you will know them. (Matthew 7:15–20)

The Christian woman who is striving to be a genuine disciple of her Lord will study His Word, imitate His ways, abide in His presence and obey His word. And as a result, she will bear good fruit. She will display the character of a true disciple, which is the character of Christ Himself.

THE VIRTUES OF DISCIPLESHIP

Throughout the teaching of Christ there are several virtues that He repeatedly inculcates upon His disciples. In fact, we could say that these virtues are the essence of a disciple's character.

The first is *humility*. Again and again Jesus taught His followers that contrary to the notions of the world, Christian virtue is rooted in this fundamental trait of humility:

> At that time the disciples came to Jesus, saying,
> "Who then is greatest in the kingdom of heaven?"
> Then Jesus called a little child to Him, set him in
> the midst of them, and said, "Assuredly, I say to
> you, unless you are converted and become as little
> children, you will by no means enter the kingdom of
> heaven. Therefore whoever humbles himself as this
> little child is the greatest in the kingdom of heaven.
> Whoever receives one little child like this in My
> name receives Me. (Matthew 18:1–5)

The disciples, being somewhat obtuse, didn't quite understand the importance of humility. Indeed, even on the eve of Christ's death, they argued about who should be greatest. James and John even lobbied to get the highest positions in the kingdom. Yet Jesus answered with a lesson on humility:

> Then James and John, the sons of Zebedee, came
> to Him, saying, "Teacher, we want You to do for
> us whatever we ask." And He said to them, "What
> do you want Me to do for you?" They said to Him,
> "Grant us that we may sit, one on Your right hand
> and the other on Your left, in Your glory." But Jesus
> said to them, "You do not know what you ask. Are
> you able to drink the cup that I drink, and be bap-
> tized with the baptism that I am baptized with?"
> They said to Him, "We are able." So Jesus said to
> them, "You will indeed drink the cup that I drink,

and with the baptism I am baptized with you will be baptized; but to sit on My right hand and on My left is not Mine to give, but it is for those for whom it is prepared." And when the ten heard it, they began to be greatly displeased with James and John. But Jesus called them to Himself and said to them, "You know that those who are considered rulers over the Gentiles lord it over them, and their great ones exercise authority over them. Yet it shall not be so among you; but whoever desires to become great among you shall be your servant. And whoever of you desires to be first shall be slave of all. For even the Son of Man did not come to be served, but to serve, and to give His life a ransom for many." (Mark 10:35–45)

A. B. Bruce, commenting on this passage, observed:

> We know how much of the world's spirit is to be found at all time in religious circles of high reputation for zeal, devotion, and sanctity, . . . We are not surprised at the behaviour of the two sons of Zebedee, and yet we say plainly that their request was foolish and offensive: indicative at once of bold presumption, gross stupidity, and unmitigated self-ishness. It was an irreverent, presumptuous request, because it virtually asked Jesus their Lord to become the tool of their ambition and vanity.[7]

"Ambition and vanity"—now there is a good definition of what moves the heart of the immodest woman. True Christian humility, on the other hand, seeks neither place nor praise. It is opposed to the pride and vanity displayed in immodesty. It is surely no coincidence that the very word *modest* may also be defined as "humility" or "reticence." It is the reluctance to advance oneself, to put oneself on display, or to promote oneself.

Another trait of a true disciple is *self-denial*. At the heart of the Christian message is the Cross. For Christ, the cross was literal—a tree of execution. And He, on the cross, bore the sins of the world. Thus the cross of Christ is the grand display of God's justice and His love: His just punishment of sin, but His great love for the sinner. And those who embrace that cross, those who believe that Christ died on that cross for their sins, are forgiven of their sins and restored to a right relationship with God.

Yet Christ's disciples have a cross of their own. It is the cross of self-denial.

> If anyone comes to Me and does not hate his father
> and mother, wife and children, brothers and sisters,
> yes, and his own life also, he cannot be My disciple.
> And whoever does not bear his cross and come
> after Me cannot be My disciple. For which of you,
> intending to build a tower, does not sit down first
> and count the cost, whether he has enough to fin-
> ish it—lest, after he has laid the foundation, and is
> not able to finish, all who see it begin to mock him,
> saying, "This man began to build and was not able
> to finish." Or what king, going to make war against
> another king, does not sit down first and consider
> whether he is able with ten thousand to meet him
> who comes against him with twenty thousand? Or
> else, while the other is still a great way off, he sends
> a delegation and asks conditions of peace. So like-
> wise, whoever of you does not forsake all that he has
> cannot be My disciple. (Luke 14:26–33)

These are tough words from a tender Savior. But there

is no way to sugarcoat the message of genuine Christian discipleship. If being a virtuous Christian were easy, we would see a lot more virtue in the church. But it's not easy and never will be. When Jesus calls us to Himself, He is calling us to become part of His church, His bride. And Christ will not play second fiddle to other lovers. He calls us to a relationship with Him that demands total surrender and total allegiance. We must put Him first before all other persons and all other desires. The woman who chooses to follow Jesus will, out of love for Him, deny her own desire. She will deny her desire for attention, her craving for applause, her lust for admiration. Looking upon His cross, she will take up her cross. Gazing upon His cross, she will turn the gaze of others toward Christ.

THE TRANSFORMING SPIRIT

The call to total surrender, complete consecration, and sacrificial cross-bearing discipleship is a call to do the impossible. Or better yet, it's a call to the supernatural. For none of us can live the Christian life, as it is supposed to be lived, in our own power. However, God has given us His Spirit to dwell in us, and it is the Holy Spirit who ultimately empowers us and transforms us. Apart from Him, we can do nothing.

It is striking that in the epistle to the Romans the Holy Spirit is mentioned only one time in the first seven chapters. And it is toward the end of chapter 7 that we see the apostle Paul's desperate cry of frustration: "O wretched man that I am! Who will deliver me from this body of death?" All of his efforts to obey the law of God and to do the will of God were in vain. He was not able to overcome indwelling sin. The power of the flesh conquered him. Strive as he might, victory eluded him. He wrestled, but in vain. Then, when finally at the point of real desperation, he ceased his own efforts and cried out for divine help. Then, and only then, do we learn the glorious secret of sanctification. For in chapter 8 of Romans, the Holy Spirit is mentioned *nineteen times*. He is the divine person of the Trinity purchased by Christ's death to take residence in our hearts and transform the very depths of our souls. His proper name and essential property are holy; for He is the One whose primary work is to make the Christian holy by transforming the soul into the moral image of Jesus Christ. Only the Holy Spirit can save and sanctify the soul, renew and transform the mind, and inspire and empower dedication. Christ died on the cross so that "the righteous requirement of the law might be fulfilled in us who do not walk according to the flesh but *according to the Spirit*" (Romans 8:4, emphasis added).

Thus, the virtue of modesty will be a fruit of the Spirit's work in our hearts. And if we want to experience His power in our lives, we must consider four apostolic exhortations regarding the Spirit. Two are negative and two are positive.

The first one is: "Do *not grieve* the Spirit." Grieving the Spirit means that we cause the Spirit pain by harboring any known sin, but especially by harboring sins of bitterness and anger. All anger, clamor, and bitterness must be put away. But notice that it is put away *from* us, not *by* us. It is the Spirit, not us, who will put these sins away from us if we will yield to His work in us. It is when we resist this work that we grieve Him. If we yield, however, He will mortify our sins and produce in us the precious fruit of the Spirit.

Also, we must *not quench* the Spirit (1 Thessalonians 5:19). Whereas grieving the Spirit has to do with practicing sin, quenching the Spirit is a result of two very specific attitudes: ingratitude and unbelief. The context of the passage makes it clear that we are to continually demonstrate a grateful attitude by expressing thanks to God. No murmuring or complaining; no whining or self-pity. Moreover, when hearing the Word shared or taught we are not to "despise prophecies" (1 Thessalonians 5:20). In other words, we must not make light of, or ignore, the Spirit's instruction and conviction coming to us through the spoken Word. If we do so, we are quenching His work. Listen to what the Spirit is saying to you through the Word. Be quiet and listen.

On the positive side, we are told first, to "be filled with the Spirit" (Ephesians 5:18) and to "walk in the Spirit" (Galatians 5:16). The filling of the Spirit happens when we practice both personal and corporate praise and worship. We are to make it a practice not only to be grateful in our hearts, but also to sing our praises—to "offer the sacrifice of praise to God, that is, the fruit of our lips, giving thanks to His name" (Hebrews 13:15). As we discipline ourselves to be grateful, the Spirit is pleased to fill our lives, as the glory filled the temple. With His presence real in our lives, the fruit of the Spirit is produced in us. And we "walk in the Spirit" by yielding to His guidance and permitting Him to manifest His fruit in us. We literally "keep step" with the Spirit.

Much more could be said about God's work of sanctification. Indeed, entire tomes have been written on it. But as it relates to our subject, Christian women must understand that the virtue of modesty is a fruit of a surrendered, sanctified, and spiritual life. Simply changing wardrobes is not God's ideal. Yes, He wants a modest dress and demeanor. But more than that, He wants a yielded will. Yield to Him and He will renew your mind, transform your soul, and sanctify your affections. Then, and only then, will you know the meaning of beauty and gain the virtue of modesty.

Afterword
Modesty and Men

When Wendy Shalit released her book, A Return to Modesty, feminists attacked her for supposedly encouraging a return to the notorious "double standard." They apparently thought Shalit was suggesting that the modern abuse of women was really the women's fault, a variation on the "blame the rape victim" mentality. Of course, Shalit said nothing of the sort.

Likewise, it would be a great mistake to assume that because we have been primarily addressing women modesty is not a male issue. On the contrary, everything we have said applies to men *in principle*. There is no double standard in the Bible. Men, just like women, must also be modest in dress, demeanor, and desire. Men must see their bodies as a gift of God to be used for His glory and not as a lure for temptation. It seems that today men are also increasingly being urged to be "sexy." They have to have those "steel abs" to show off to the ladies, you know. Thus, just as with women, men are being pressured to view their bodies as sexual bait. It's all about "the bod." Men must beware of immodest actions and words. Men must culti-vate self-control, purity, and propriety. There is no double standard when it comes to holiness.

Men are also being pressured to be more feminine. Not only is there the push to be more "affectional," but men's fashions are mimicking female styles. The push for androgyny is strong. In particular, we see men wear-ing more jewelry, sporting tattoos, and even piercing their ears (and perhaps their eyebrows and tongues). How should Christian men respond to all this?

First, we must look at the Scripture. Regarding the practice of marking the body, there is a clear biblical prohibition against cutting the flesh (Leviticus 21:5). A tattoo is exactly that: it is a mark on the body made by cutting or burning. But we also need to remember what we said about "association." This applies to more than just clothing or brand names. A Christian man needs to see the piercing phenomenon in terms of its message: it is a pseudo-religious mark of ownership. In a way, it is a nihilistic version of Christian baptism. It is an attempt to "mark" oneself in order to identify with a community, phi-losophy, or way of life. So, the question to ask yourself is this: Do I want to identify with pagan nihilism? Of course, a young man might reply, "But I don't mean *that* by my tattoo." Perhaps not. But the association still stands, and what he must see is that other people will read his mark in light of their worldview and culture. His mark sends a message, and he must be responsible for what he is saying.

What about the rage for rings? Is an earring or a nose ring okay? Again, we must look at the Word and look at our culture. In the Bible, piercing is a mark of subordination, and thus it is permissible for a woman, who is sub-ordinate to her husband, to have her ear or nose pierced. However, whenever we read in the Bible of men with ear-rings, they have "either just come out of slavery or were just going into it. Body piercing is a mark of slavery."[1] Thus, in the Old Testament culture, piercing the ear was associated with subordination; but what does it mean in ours? That is the question to answer. For once you answer that question (and answer it honestly), then you will be in a position to know whether it is permissible to wear rings. What John Makujina says of clothing in general applies to jewelry in particular:

> Because symbols are dynamic rather than static,
> they can take on new meaning. It may be that after
> a period of time certain less obvious counter-culture
> items will become so commonplace that they will
> no longer signify rebellion or moral deviance, but
> will be acceptable at every level of society. Until,
> and *if*, this happens, those symbols on Christians
> would still carry their original negative overtones,
> whatever they may be. Therefore, with items of
> clothing that do not carry intrinsic messages of
> indecency, . . . the social and moral meaning of the
> article should be carefully considered within the
> context of culture and avoided if it diverges from
> Christian values.[2]

Modesty applies to men in yet another way. Through-out *The Beauty of Modesty*, we have urged women to be mindful of the male's fascination with the female form. We have urged women to be modest in light of male lust. This is right and good. But the real problem is the male himself. Men do have a problem with lust, and it is their responsibility to conquer it. There is a simple law in economics called the law of "supply and demand." Advertisers spend billions of dollars a year trying to create a "demand" for products. Well, as it relates to modesty, it is the men who are creating the demand. It is men who are buying and viewing the pornography. It is men who like the show and, therefore, are doing nothing to halt our slide into moral perversion. If men did not lust, women would not be disrobing. It's really that simple.

So, if we want to create a culture of modesty, at least in our churches, men will have to master their passions. This means repenting of all sexual immorality, even in our thought lives, and disciplining ourselves to conquer the beast within. In short, it means practical sanctification: being in the Word, in prayer, in fellowship, and being accountable. Everything that we have already said about the Cross and self-denial applies here also. Mortification is painful, but if we want victory, we will have to pay the price. It's all a question of how badly we want it. We will get just as much victory as we really want.

Last, modesty is a male issue because a man is ultimately responsible for the condition of his wife and children. We have already mentioned this also, but it cannot be overemphasized. In a Christian home, the father is the covenantal head. This means that just as Christ took upon Himself the sins of His people, likewise, the father assumes full responsibility for those in his household. When we see a young girl sporting skintight hip-huggers and a see-through blouse, we ought to ask: "Where is her father? Why is he letting his daughter dress like a hooker?" Well, he is probably letting her dress that way because he doesn't want the hassle of fighting with her. In other words, he is a wimp. The real problem, of course, is spiritual. His daughter (or wife) wants to look that way, and that is a sign of a problem, a problem he has a responsibility to address.

Much more could be said, but if the heart is right and the principles are clear, then application is all that is needed. A man must start with himself, his own lustful heart, and get victory there. Then he must assume the mantle at home and see that he is nurturing and protecting his wife and children. In sum, he must be mature and responsible. No more of this "boys will be boys" stuff. It's time for the boys to be men.

Appendix
MODEST PROPOSALS

Our concern about modesty in the church and culture is nothing new. Christian thinkers down through the ages have always been concerned that feminine beauty and modesty be reflected in the church. In addition to the quotations sprinkled throughout *The Beauty of Modesty*, we thought it might be helpful to have a further sampling of what others have said about modesty. This section might also serve as a valuable resource for pastors or leaders who intend to teach on modesty.

Tertullian: On the Apparel of Women

That salvation [of which I speak] consists in the exhibition principally of modesty. For since, by the introduction into a consecration of the Holy Spirit [in us], we are all "the temple of God," modesty is the sacristan and priestess of the temple, who is to suffer nothing unclean or profane to be introduced into it, for fear that the God who inhabits it should be offended and quite forsake the polluted abode.

How many a one, in short, is there who does not earnestly desire even to look pleasing to stranger" who does not on that very account take care to have herself painted out, and denies that she has ever been an object of carnal appetite: And yet, granting that even this is a practice familiar to Gentile modesty—namely, not actually to commit the sin, but still to be willing to do so. . . . For all things which are not God's are perverse. Let those women therefore look to it, who by not holding fast the whole good, easily mingle with evil even what they do hold fast. Necessary it is that you turn aside from them, as in all other things, so also in your gait; since you ought to be "perfect, as is your Father who is in the heavens."

You know that in the eye of perfect, that is, Christian modesty, carnal desire of one's self on the part of others is not only not to be desired, but even execrated, by you. . . . Why therefore excite toward yourself that evil passion? Why invite that to which you profess yourself a stranger? . . . We ought not to open a way to temptations, which, by their instancy, sometimes achieve a wickedness which God expels from them who are His; or, at all events, put the spirit into a thorough tumult by presenting a stumbling-block.

Let a holy woman, if naturally beautiful, give none so great occasion for carnal appetite. Certainly, if even she be so, she ought not to set off her beauty, but even to veil it.

What "grace" is compatible with "injury"? What "beauty" with "impurities"?

For where God is, there modesty is. . . .

How, then, shall we practice modesty without her instrumental means, that is, without sobriety? How, moreover, shall we bring sobriety to bear on the discharge of the function of modesty, unless seriousness in appearance and in countenance, and in the general aspect of the entire man, mark our carriage?

To Christian modesty it is not enough to *be* so, but to *seem* so too. For so great ought its plentitude to be, that it may flow out from the mind to the garb, and burst out from the conscience to the outward appearance. . . .

Clothe yourselves with the silk of uprightness, the fine linen of holiness, the purple of modesty. Thus painted, you will have God as your Lover.

Appendix

Ambrose: Duties of Clergy

Lovely, then, is the virtue of modesty, and sweet is its grace! It is seen not only in actions, but even in our words, so that we may not go beyond due measure in speech, and that our words may not have an unbecoming sound. The mirror of our mind often enough reflects its image in our words.

For modesty is the companion of purity, in company with which chastity itself is safer. Shame, again, is good as a companion and guide of chastity, inasmuch as it does not suffer purity to be defiled in approaching even the outskirts of danger.

Modesty must further be guarded in our very movements and gestures and gait. The condition of the mind is often seen in the attitude of the body.

Modesty has indeed its rocks—not any that she brings with her, but those, I mean, which she often runs against, as when we associate with profligate men, who, under the form of pleasantry, administer poison to the good.

Martin Luther: Larger Catechism (on the Sixth Commandment)

These commandments now [that follow] are easily understood from [the explanation of] the preceding; for they are all to the effect that we [be careful to] avoid doing any kind of injury to our neighbor. But they are arranged in fine [elegant] order. In the first place, they treat of his own person. Then they proceed to the person nearest him, or the closest possession next after his body namely, his wife, who is one flesh and blood with him, so that we cannot inflict a higher injury upon him in any good that is his. Therefore it is explicitly forbidden here to bring any disgrace upon him in respect to his wife. And it really aims at adultery, because among the Jews it was ordained and commanded that every one must be married. Therefore also the young were early provided for [married], so that the virgin state was held in small esteem, neither were public prostitution and lewdness tolerated (as now). Therefore adultery was the most common form of unchastity among them.

But because among us there is such a shameful mess and the very dregs of all vice and lewdness, this commandment is directed also against all manner of unchastity, whatever it may be called; and not only is the external act forbidden, but also every kind of cause, incitement, and means, so that the heart, the lips, and the whole body may be chaste and afford no opportunity, help, or persuasion to unchastity. And not only this, but that we also make resistance, afford protection and rescue wherever there is danger and need; and again, that we give help and counsel, so as to maintain our neighbor's honor. For whenever you omit this when you could make resistance, or connive at it as if it did not concern you, you are as truly guilty as the one perpetrating the deed. Thus, to state it in the briefest manner, there is required this much, that every one both live chastely himself and help his neighbor do the same, so that God by this commandment wishes to hedge round about and protect [as with a rampart] every spouse that no one trespass against them.

Therefore God has also most richly blessed this estate [marriage] above all others, and, in addition, has bestowed on it and wrapped up in it everything in the world, to the end that this estate might be well and richly provided for. Married life is therefore no jest or presumption; but it is an excellent thing and a matter of divine seriousness. For it is of the highest importance to Him that persons be raised who may serve the world and promote the knowledge of God, godly living, and all virtues, to fight against wickedness and the devil.

Therefore I have always taught that this estate should not be despised nor held in disrepute, as is done by the blind world and our false ecclesiastics, but that it be regarded according to God's Word, by which it is adorned and sanctified, so that it is not only placed on an equality with other estates, but that it precedes and surpasses them all, whether they be that of emperor, princes, bishops, or whoever they please. For both ecclesiastical and civil estates must humble themselves and all be found in this estate as we shall hear. Therefore it is not a peculiar estate, but the most common and noblest estate, which pervades all Christendom, yea, which extends through all the world.

Now, I speak of this in order that the young may be so guided that they conceive a liking for the married estate, and know that it is a blessed estate and pleasing to God. For in this way we might in the course of time bring it about that married life be restored to honor, and that there might be less of the filthy, dissolute, disorderly doings which now run riot the world over in open prostitution and other shameful vices arising from disregard of married life. Therefore it is the duty of parents and the government to see to it that our youth be brought up to discipline and respectability, and when they have come to years of maturity, to provide for them [to have them married] in the fear of God and honorably; He would not fail to add His blessing and grace, so that men would have joy and happiness from the same.

Let me now say in conclusion that this commandment demands not only that every one live chastely in thought, word, and deed in his condition, that is, especially in the estate of matrimony, but also that every one love and esteem the spouse given him by God. For where conjugal chastity is to be maintained, man and wife must by all means live together in love and harmony, that one may cherish the other from the heart and with entire fidelity. For that is one of the principal points which enkindle love and desire of chastity, so that, where this is found, chastity will follow as a matter of course without any command. Therefore also St. Paul so diligently exhorts husband and wife to love and honor one another. Here you have again a precious, yea, many and great good works, of which you can joyfully boast, against all ecclesiastical estates, chosen without God's Word and commandment.

Heidelberg Catechism: Question 109
Question: Does God forbid in this commandment, only adul-

tery, and such like gross sins?

Answer: Since both our body and soul are temples of the holy Ghost, he commands us to preserve them pure and holy: therefore he forbids all unchaste actions, gestures, words, thoughts, desires, and whatever can entice men thereto.

Zacharius Ursinus: On the Fifth Commandment

Modesty is a virtue closely allied to gravity, which, from a knowledge of our own weakness, and from a consideration of the office and position which we occupy by divine appointment, maintains consistency and propriety in actions and deportment of life, regardless of the opinions and remarks which men may make and entertain respecting us, with this design, that we do not arrogate to ourselves more than is becoming, or defraud others of the respect and honor due them; that we do not make a greater display in our apparel, walk, conversation and life, than is proper and needful; that we do not esteem ourselves more lightly than others, or oppress them; but maintain a deportment according to our ability and strength, with an acknowledgment of God's gifts in others, and of our faults and imperfections. This and the former virtue [gravity] are, as has just been remarked, closely allied; for gravity without being joined with modesty, soon degenerates into ambition and haughtiness. "For if a man think himself to be something when he is nothing, he deceives himself" (Galatians 6:3). Humility and modesty differ from each other in this, that modesty is directed towards men, and consists in acknowledging our own faults and the gifts that others are possessed; whilst humility has respect to God.

The following vices are opposed to this virtue: 1. Immodesty, which transcend the bounds of propriety in the words, actions and deportment of the life, both as it respects ourselves, and those with whom we hold daily intercourse. 2. Arrogance, which in conceit and outward declaration takes to itself more than it really possesses, or admires its own gifts and boasts of them beyond measure. 3. A counterfeiting or mere show of modesty, which evinces itself in the admiration which any one has of himself, whilst he, nevertheless, feigns to be backward in accepting of honors and offices, which he all the while desires, in order that he may advance his own praise and conceit of modesty.

Westminster Larger Catechism: Questions 137–139

Question 137: Which is the seventh commandment?

Answer: The seventh commandment is, Thou shalt not commit adultery.

Question 138: What are the duties required in the seventh commandment?

Answer: The duties required in the seventh commandment are, chastity in body, mind, affections, words, and behavior; and the preservation of it in ourselves and others; watchfulness over the eyes and all the senses; temperance, keeping of chaste company, modesty in apparel; marriage by those that have not the gift of continency, conjugal love, and cohabitation; diligent labor in our callings; shunning all occasions of uncleanness, and resisting temptations thereunto.

Question 139: What are the sins forbidden in the seventh commandment?

Answer: The sins forbidden in the seventh commandment, besides the neglect of the duties required, are, adultery, fornication, rape, incest, sodomy, and all unnatural lusts; all unclean imaginations, thoughts, purposes, and affections; all corrupt or filthy communications, or listening thereunto; wanton looks, impudent or light behavior, immodest apparel; prohibiting of lawful, and dispensing with unlawful marriages; allowing, tolerating, keeping of stews, and resorting to them; entangling vows of single life, undue delay of marriage; having more wives or husbands than one at the same time; unjust divorce, or desertion; idleness, gluttony, drunkenness, unchaste company; lascivious songs, books, pictures, dancings, stage plays; and all other provocations to, or acts of uncleanness, either in ourselves or others.

Thomas Aquinas: Summa Theologica

Second Part of the Second Part (Questions 1–189) Question 169: Of Modesty in the Outward Apparel (Two Articles)

We must now consider modesty as connected with the outward apparel, and under this head there are two points of inquiry:

(1) Whether there can be virtue and vice in connection with outward apparel?

(2) Whether women sin mortally by excessive adornment?

Whether there can be virtue and vice in connection with outward apparel?

Objection 1: It would seem that there cannot be virtue and vice in connection with outward apparel. For outward adornment does not belong to us by nature, wherefore it varies according to different times and places. Hence Augustine says (De Doctr. Christ. iii, 12) that "among the ancient Romans it was scandalous for one to wear a cloak with sleeves and reaching to the ankles, whereas now it is scandalous for anyone hailing from a reputable place to be without them." Now according to the Philosopher (Ethic. ii, 1) there is in us a natural aptitude for the virtues. Therefore there is no virtue or vice about such things.

Objection 2: Further, if there were virtue and vice in connection with outward attire, excess in this matter would be sinful. Now excess in outward attire is not apparently sinful, since even the ministers of the altar use most precious vestments in the sacred ministry. Likewise it would seem not to be sinful to be lacking in this, for it is said in praise of certain people (Hebrews 11:37): "They wandered about in sheepskins and in goatskins." Therefore it seems that there cannot be virtue and vice in this matter.

Objection 3: Further, every virtue is either theological, or moral, or intellectual. Now an intellectual virtue is not conversant with matter of this kind, since it is a perfection regarding the knowledge of truth. Nor is there a theological virtue connected therewith, since that has God for its object; nor are any of the moral virtues enumerated by the Philosopher (Ethic. ii, 7), connected with it. Therefore it seems that there cannot be virtue and vice in connection with this kind of attire.

On the contrary, Honesty pertains to virtue. Now a certain honesty is observed in the outward apparel; for Ambrose says (De Offic. i, 19): "The body should be bedecked naturally and without affectation, with simplicity, with negligence rather than nicety, not with costly and dazzling apparel, but with ordinary clothes, so that nothing be lacking to honesty and necessity, yet nothing be added to increase its beauty." Therefore there can be virtue and vice in the outward attire.

I answer that, It is not in the outward things themselves which man uses, that there is vice, but on the part of man who uses them immoderately. This lack of moderation occurs in two ways. First, in comparison with the customs of those among whom one lives; wherefore Augustine says (Confess. iii, 8): "Those offenses which are contrary to the customs of men, are to be avoided according to the customs generally prevailing, so that a thing agreed upon and confirmed by custom or law of any city or nation may not be violated at the lawless pleasure of any, whether citizen or foreigner. For any part, which harmonizeth not with its whole, is offensive." Secondly, the lack of moderation in the use of these things may arise from the inordinate attachment of the user, the result being that a man sometimes takes too much pleasure in using them, either in accordance with the custom of those among whom he dwells or contrary to such custom. Hence Augustine says (De Doctr. Christ. iii, 12): "We must avoid excessive pleasure in the use of things, for it leads not only wickedly to abuse the customs of those among whom we dwell, but frequently to exceed their bounds, so that, whereas it lay hidden, while under the restraint of established morality, it displays its deformity in a most lawless outbreak."

In point of excess, this inordinate attachment occurs in three ways. First when a man seeks glory from excessive attention to dress; in so far as dress and such like things are a kind of ornament. Hence Gregory says (Hom. xl in Ev.): "There are some who think that attention to finery and costly dress is no sin. Surely, if this were no fault, the word of God would not say so expressly that the rich man who was tortured in hell had been clothed in purple and fine linen. No one, forsooth, seeks costly apparel" (such, namely, as exceeds his estate) "save for vainglory." Secondly, when a man seeks sensuous pleasure from excessive attention to dress, in so far as dress is directed to the body's comfort. Thirdly, when a man is too solicitous in his attention to outward apparel.

Accordingly Andronicus reckons three virtues in connection with outward attire; namely "humility," which excludes the seeking of glory, wherefore he says that humility is "the habit of avoiding excessive expenditure and parade"; "contentment," which excludes the seeking of sensuous pleasure, wherefore he says that "contentedness is the habit that makes a man satisfied with what is suitable, and enables him to determine what is becoming in his manner of life" (according to the saying of the Apostle, 1 Timothy 6:8): "Having food and wherewith to be covered, with these let us be content";—and "simplicity," which excludes excessive solicitude about such things, wherefore he says that "simplicity is a habit that makes a man contented with what he has."

In the point of deficiency there may be inordinate attachment in two ways. First, through a man's neglect to give the requisite study or trouble to the use of outward apparel. Wherefore the Philosopher says (Ethic. vii, 7) that "it is a mark of effeminacy to let one's cloak trail on the ground to avoid the trouble of lifting it up." Secondly, by seeking glory from the very lack of attention to outward attire. Hence Augustine says (De Serm. Dom. in Monte ii, 12) that "not only the glare and pomp of outward things, but even dirt and the weeds of mourning may be a subject of ostentation, all the more dangerous as being a decoy under the guise of God's service"; and the Philosopher says (Ethic. iv, 7) that "both excess and inordinate defect are a subject of ostentation."

Reply to Objection 1: Although outward attire does not come from nature, it belongs to natural reason to moderate it; so that we are naturally inclined to be the recipients of the virtue that moderates outward raiment.

Reply to Objection 2: Those who are placed in a position of dignity, or again the ministers of the altar, are attired in more costly apparel than others, not for the sake of their own glory, but to indicate the excellence of their office or of the Divine worship: wherefore this is not sinful in them. Hence Augustine says (De Doctr. Christ. iii, 12): "Whoever uses outward things in such a way as to exceed the bounds observed by the good people among whom he dwells, either signifies something by so doing, or is guilty of sin, inasmuch as he uses these things for sensual pleasure or ostentation."

Likewise there may be sin on the part of deficiency: although it is not always a sin to wear coarser clothes than other people. For, if this be done through ostentation or pride, in order to set oneself above others, it is a sin of superstition; whereas, if this be done to tame the flesh, or to humble the spirit, it belongs to the virtue of temperance. Hence Augustine says (De Doctr. Christ. iii, 12): "Whoever uses transitory things with greater restraint than is customary with those among whom he dwells, is either temperate or superstitious." Especially, however, is the use of coarse raiment befitting to those who by word and example urge others to repentance, as did the prophets of whom the Apostle is speaking in the passage quoted. Wherefore a gloss on Matthew 3:4, says: "He who preaches penance, wears the garb of penance."

Reply to Objection 3: This outward apparel is an indication of man's estate; wherefore excess, deficiency, and mean therein, are referable to the virtue of truthfulness, which the Philosopher

(Ethic. ii, 7) assigns to deeds and words, which are indications of something connected with man's estate.

Whether the adornment of women is devoid of mortal sin?

Objection 1: It would seem that the adornment of women is not devoid of mortal sin. For whatever is contrary to a precept of the Divine law is a mortal sin. Now the adornment of women is contrary to a precept of the Divine law; for it is written (1 Peter 3:3): "Whose," namely women's, "adorning, let it not be the outward plaiting of the hair, or the wearing of gold, or the putting on of apparel." Wherefore a gloss of Cyprian says: "Those who are clothed in silk and purple cannot sincerely put on Christ: those who are bedecked with gold and pearls and trinkets have forfeited the adornments of mind and body." Now this is not done without a mortal sin. Therefore the adornment of women cannot be devoid of mortal sin.

Objection 2: Further, Cyprian says (De Habit. Virg.): "I hold that not only virgins and widows, but also wives and all women without exception, should be admonished that nowise should they deface God's work and fabric, the clay that He has fashioned, with the aid of yellow pigments, black powders or rouge, or by applying any dye that alters the natural features." And afterwards he adds: "They lay hands on God, when they strive to reform what He has formed. This is an assault on the Divine handiwork, a distortion of the truth. Thou shalt not be able to see God, having no longer the eyes that God made, but those the devil has unmade; with him shalt thou burn on whose account thou art bedecked." But this is not due except to mortal sin. Therefore the adornment of women is not devoid of mortal sin.

Objection 3: Further, just as it is unbecoming for a woman to wear man's clothes, so is it unbecoming for her to adorn herself inordinately. Now the former is a sin, for it is written (Deuteronomy 22:5): "A woman shall not be clothed with man's apparel, neither shall a man use woman's apparel." Therefore it seems that also the excessive adornment of women is a mortal sin.

Objection 4: On the contrary, If this were true it would seem that the makers of these means of adornment sin mortally.

I answer that, As regards the adornment of women, we must bear in mind the general statements made above (Article [1]) concerning outward apparel, and also something special, namely that a woman's apparel may incite men to lust, according to Proverbs 7:10, "Behold a woman meeteth him in harlot's attire, prepared to deceive souls."

Nevertheless a woman may use means to please her husband, lest through despising her he fall into adultery. Hence it is written (1 Corinthians 7:34) that the woman "that is married thinketh on the things of the world, how she may please her husband." Wherefore if a married woman adorn herself in order to please her husband she can do this without sin.

But those women who have no husband nor wish to have one, or who are in a state of life inconsistent with marriage, cannot without sin desire to give lustful pleasure to those men who see them, because this is to incite them to sin. And if indeed they adorn themselves with this intention of provoking others to lust, they sin mortally; whereas if they do so from frivolity, or from vanity for the sake of ostentation, it is not always mortal, but sometimes venial. And the same applies to men in this respect. Hence Augustine says (Ep. ccxlv ad Possid.): "I do not wish you to be hasty in forbidding the wearing of gold or costly attire except in the case of those who being neither married nor wishful to marry, should think how they may please God: whereas the others think on the things of the world, either husbands how they may please their wives, or wives how they may please their husbands, except that it is unbecoming for women though married to uncover their hair, since the Apostle commands them to cover the head." Yet in this case some might be excused from sin, when they do this not through vanity but on account of some contrary custom: although such a custom is not to be commended.

Reply to Objection 1: As a gloss says on this passage, "The

wives of those who were in distress despised their husbands, and decked themselves that they might please other men": and the Apostle forbids this. Cyprian is speaking in the same sense; yet he does not forbid married women to adorn themselves in order to please their husbands, lest the latter be afforded an occasion of sin with other women. Hence the Apostle says (1 Timothy 2:9): "Women . . . in ornate [Douay: 'decent'] apparel, adorning themselves with modesty and sobriety, not with plaited hair, or gold, or pearls, or costly attire": whence we are given to understand that women are not forbidden to adorn themselves soberly and moderately but to do so excessively, shamelessly, and immodestly.

Reply to Objection 2: Cyprian is speaking of women painting themselves: this is a kind of falsification, which cannot be devoid of sin. Wherefore Augustine says (Ep. ccxlv ad Possid.): "To dye oneself with paints in order to have a rosier or a paler complexion is a lying counterfeit. I doubt whether even their husbands are willing to be deceived by it, by whom alone" (i.e. the husbands) "are they to be permitted, but not ordered, to adorn themselves." However, such painting does not always involve a mortal sin, but only when it is done for the sake of sensuous pleasure or in contempt of God, and it is to like cases that Cyprian refers.

It must, however, be observed that it is one thing to counterfeit a beauty one has not, and another to hide a disfigurement arising from some cause such as sickness or the like. For this is lawful, since according to the Apostle (1 Corinthians 12:23), "such as we think to be the less honorable members of the body, about these we put more abundant honor."

Reply to Objection 3: As stated in the foregoing Article, outward apparel should be consistent with the estate of the person, according to the general custom. Hence it is in itself sinful for a woman to wear man's clothes, or vice versa; especially since this may be a cause of sensuous pleasure; and it is expressly forbidden in the Law (Deuteronomy 22) because the Gentiles

used to practice this change of attire for the purpose of idolatrous superstition. Nevertheless this may be done sometimes
without sin on account of some necessity, either in order to hide
oneself from enemies, or through lack of other clothes, or for
some similar motive.

Reply to Objection 4: In the case of an art directed to the
production of goods which men cannot use without sin, it follows that the workmen sin in making such things, as directly
affording others an occasion of sin; for instance, if a man were
to make idols or anything pertaining to idolatrous worship. But
in the case of an art the products of which may be employed
by man either for a good or for an evil use, such as swords,
arrows, and the like, the practice of such an art is not sinful.
These alone should be called arts; wherefore Chrysostom says:
"The name of art should be applied to those only which con-
tribute towards and produce necessaries and mainstays of life."
In the case of an art that produces things which for the most
part some people put to an evil use, although such arts are not
unlawful in themselves, nevertheless, according to the teaching
of Plato, they should be extirpated from the State by the gov-
erning authority. Accordingly, since women may lawfully adorn
themselves, whether to maintain the fitness of their estate, or
even by adding something thereto, in order to please their husbands, it follows that those who make such means of adornment
do not sin in the practice of their art, except perhaps by invent-
ing means that are superfluous and fantastic. Hence Chrysostom
says (Super Matth.) that "even the shoemakers' and clothiers'
arts stand in need of restraint, for they have lent their art to lust,
by abusing its needs, and debasing art by art."

John Newton: On Female Dress

Few ministers touch upon this subject [modesty] in their public
discourses; and indeed it is not very easy to treat it with propriety from the pulpit. Yet whatever is unsuitable to the Christian
profession, an inlet to temptation and productive of evil conse-

quences, should in some way or other be noticed, by those who have the honour of the gospel, and the welfare of their fellow-creatures at heart.

. . . An unaffected neatness, according to different situations in life, seems a tolerable definition of a becoming dress.

If clothes are considered merely as a covering for the body, and defence from the cold, it will be difficult to draw the line, and to determine exactly between what is necessary, and what is superfluous.

. . . And it is more for the honour of the gospel, that a woman professing godliness should be distinguished from others, by modesty, sobriety, and good works, than by the shape of her cap, or the colour of her garment.

But a nice attention to dress will cost you much of what is more valuable than money,—your precious time. It will too much occupy your thoughts, and that at the seasons when you would wish to have them otherwise engaged. And it certainly administers fuel to that latent fire of pride and vanity, which is inseparable from our fallen nature, and is easily blown up into a blaze.

If a woman, when going to public worship, looks in the glass, and contemplates, with a secret self-complacence, the figure which it reflects to her view, I am afraid she is not in the frame of spirit most suitable for one, who is about to cry for mercy as a miserable sinner.

If some allowance is to be made for youth on this head, it is painful to see others, and possibly sometimes grandmothers, who seem, by the gaudiness and levity of their attire, very unwilling to be sensible that they are growing older.

We are required to attend to the things that are lovely and of a good report. Every willful deviation from this rule is sinful. Why should a godly woman, or one who wishes to be thought so, make herself ridiculous, or hazard a suspicion of her character, to please and imitate an ungodly world?

But the worst of all the fashions are those, which are evidently calculated to allure the eyes, and to draw the attention of our [the male] sex. . . . They are indeed noticed by the men, but not to their honour nor advantage. The manner of their dress gives encouragement to vile and insidious men, and exposes them to dangerous temptations. . . . But honest and sensible men regard their exterior, as a warning signal, not to choose a companion for life, from among persons of this light and volatile turn of mind.

Robert Hall: Modern Infidelity Considered

Of all the vices incident to human nature, the most destructive to society are vanity, ferocity, and unbridled sensuality; and these are precisely the vices which infidelity is calculated to cherish.

It [vanity] forms the heart to such a profound indifference to the welfare of others, that . . . you will infallibly find the vain man is his own center. Attentive only to himself . . . he considers life as a stage on which he is performing a part, and mankind in no other light than spectators.

Settle it therefore in your minds, as a maxim never to be effaced or forgotten, that atheism is an inhuman, bloody, ferocious system, equally hostile to very useful restraint, and to every virtuous affection; that leaving nothing above us to excite awe, nor round us to awaken tenderness, it wages war with heaven and with earth: its first object is to dethrone God, its next to destroy man.

The benevolence and wisdom of the Author of Christianity are eminently conspicuous in the laws he has enacted on this branch of morals; for, while he authorizes marriage, he restrains the vagrancy and caprice of the passions, by forbidding polygamy and divorce; and, well knowing the offences against the laws of chastity usually spring from an ill-regulated imagination, he inculcates purity of heart.

Among innumerable benefits which the world has derived from the Christian religion, a superior refinement in the sexual sentiments, a more equal and respectful treatment of women, greater dignity and permanence conferred on the institution of marriage, are not the least considerable; in consequence of which the purest affections, and the most sacred duties, are grafted on the stock of the strongest instincts.

John Wesley: Sermon 88: On Dress

St. Paul exhorts all those who desire to "be transformed by the renewal of their minds," and to "prove what is that good and acceptable and perfect will of God," not to be "conformed to this world." Indeed this exhortation relates more directly to the *wisdom* of the world, which is totally opposite to his "good and acceptable and perfect will." But it likewise has a reference even to the *manners* and *customs* of the world, which naturally flow from its wisdom and spirit, and are exactly suitable thereto. And it was not beneath the wisdom of God to give us punctual directions in this respect also.

Gay and costly apparel directly tends to create and inflame lust. . . . The fact is plain and undeniable. . . . Did you not *know* this would be the natural consequence of your elegant adorning? To push the question home, Did you not *desire*, did you not *design* it should?

Let a single intention to please God prescribe both what clothing you shall buy, and the manner wherein it shall be made, and how you shall put on and wear it. To express the same thing in other words: Let all you do, in this respect, be so done that you may offer it to God, a sacrifice acceptable through Christ Jesus; so that, consequently, it may increase your reward and brighten your crown in heaven. And so it will do, if it be agreeable to Christian humility, seriousness, and charity.

John Wesley: Thoughts Upon Dress

Whoever acts with a single eye, does all things to be seen and approved of God; and can no more dress, that he can pray, or give alms, "to be seen of men."

Our carcasses will soon fall into the dust; then let the survivors adorn them with flowers. Meantime, let us regard those ornaments only that will accompany us into eternity.

What kind of persons are those to whom you could be recommended by gay or costly apparel? None that are any way likely to make you happy; this pleases only the silliest and worst of men.

Jeremy Taylor: Holy Living and Holy Dying

Be grave, decent, and modest, in thy clothing and ornament: never let it be above thy condition, not always equal to it, never light or amorous, never discovering [revealing] a nakedness through a thin veil, which thou pretendest to hide, never to lay a snare for a soul; but remember what becomes a Christian, professing holiness, chastity, and the discipline of the Holy Jesus. . . .

Hither, also, is to be reduced singular and affected walking, proud, nice, and ridiculous gestures of body, painting and lascivious dressings: all which together God reproves by the prophet (see Isaiah 3:16–18).

William Law: A Serious Call to a Devout and Holy Life

For there is nothing to be said, for the wisdom of sobriety, the wisdom of devotion, the wisdom of charity, or the wisdom of humility, but what is as good an argument for the wise and reasonable use of apparel.

If you may be vain in one thing, you may be vain in every thing; for one kind of vanity only differs from another, as one kind of intemperance differs from another.

. . . It is as impossible for a mind that is in a true state of religion, to be vain in the use of clothes, as to be vain in the use of alms, or devotions.

. . . And consequently it must be own'd, that all needless and expensive finery of dress, is the effect of a disordered heart, that is not governed by the true spirit of religion.

So that all the world agree in owning, that the use and manner of clothes is a mark of the state of a man's mind, and consequently that it is a thing highly essential to religion.

To pretend to make the way of the world our measure in

these things, is as weak and absurd, as to make the way of the world the measure of our sobriety, abstinence, or humility. It is a pretence that is exceedingly absurd in the mouths of Christians, who are to be so far from conforming to the fashions of this life, that to have overcome the world, is made an essential mark of Christianity.

If you would be a good Christian, there is but one way, you must live wholly unto God; and if you would live wholly unto God, you must live according to the wisdom that comes from God; you must act according to right judgments of the nature and value of things; you must live in the exercise of holy and heavenly affections, and use all the gifts of God to his praise and glory.

Let every one but guard against the vanity of dress, let them but make their use of clothes a matter of conscience, let them but desire to make the best use of their money, and then every one has a rule that is sufficient to direct them in every state of life.

So he that lets Religion teach him, that the end of clothing is only to hide our shame and nakedness, and to secure our bodies from the injuries of weather, and that he is to desire to glorify God by a sober and wise use of this necessity, will always know what vanity of dress is, in his particular state.

Let your dress be sober, clean, and modest, not to set out the beauty of your person, but to declare the sobriety of your mind, that your outward garb may resemble the inward plainness and simplicity of your heart. For it is highly reasonable, that you should be one man, all of a piece, and appear outwardly such as you are inwardly.

Henry Bullinger: Decades (on the Seventh Commandment)

[In the seventh commandment] all things else are forbidden, that do incite or allure us to unlawful lusts; which baits are the over-nice pranking and decking the body, evil and wanton company, gluttony, surfeiting, and drunkenness.

Men are provoked to lust either by hearing or reading of dishonest ditties and bawdy ballads, or by looking on and beholding wanton dances, unseemly sights, ribald talk, and filthy examples.

So then in this seventh precept charge is given for the maintenance of shamefacedness, modesty, sobriety, temperancy, chastity, public honesty, and true holiness of soul and body.

Our garments must be cleanly and honest, according to our country fashion, to cover and become us, unless our country fashion be too far out of order; there must be in them no hypocritical sluttishness, beyond-sea gauds, newfangled toys, nor unseemly sights.

The Chief apostles of Christ, Peter, and Paul, were not ashamed in their epistles to write somewhat largely touching the manner and ordering of women's apparel; because that kind of people do most of all bend to that foolish bravery. Let every faithful body think what is seemly for them to wear, not so much by their degree in dignity or condition of riches, as by their religion. Excess in every thing is discommended in Christians. And to what end do we jag and gash the garments that are sewed together to cover our bodies, but that thereby we may, as it were, by a most fond and ridiculous anatomy, open and lay forth to the eyes of all men what kind of people we are in our inward heart . . . ?

James Durham: The Decalogue (on the Seventh Commandment)

And whereas at first, clothing was appointed for covering nakedness, for preventing of incitements to lust and for decency; now, Jezebel-like, it is made use of to be a provocation thereunto.

And certainly men's minds are often infected with lascivious thoughts, and lustful inclinations, even by the use and sight of gaudy and vain clothing. . . .

It is both a wonderful and sad thing that women should

need to be reproved for such things, which are in themselves: 1. So gross, that, let the most innocent be enquired whence these more than ordinary discoveries do proceed, and they must at least grant that the first practicers of such a fashion could have no other design in it than the more thereby to please and allure men's carnal eyes and regards. And 2. So impudent for if to be all naked be shameful and exceedingly ready to provoke lust, must not nakedness in part, more or less, be and do the same?

There is in clothes a base effeminateness amongst men (which someway emasculates or un-mans them) who delight in those things which women dote upon, as dressing of hair, powderings, washings, rings, jewels, etc, . . .

Also interchanging of apparel is condemned; men putting on women's, and women men's clothes, which is unsuitable to that distinction of sexes which the Lord has made, and is condemned in the Word as a confusion, an absurd, unnatural thing, and an inlet to much wickedness.

Thomas Watson: Works (on the Seventh Commandment)

Look to your eyes. Much sin comes in by the eye, 2 Peter 2:14. The eye tempts the fancy, and the fancy works upon the heart. A wanton amorous eye may usher in sin. Eve first saw the tree of knowledge, and then she took, Genesis 3:6. First she looked and then she loved.

Look to your lips. Take heed of any unseemly word that may enkindle unclean thoughts in yourselves or others, 1 Corinthians 15:33. Impure discourse is the bellows to blow up the fire of lust. Much evil is conveyed to the heart by the tongue.

Look to your attire. We read of "the attire of a harlot," Proverbs 7:10. A wanton dress is a provocation to lust. Curlings and towerings of the hair, a painted face, naked breasts, are allurements to vanity. . . . Hierom says, such as by their lascivious attire endeavour to draw others to lust, though no evil follow, yet these tempters shall be punished, because they offered poison to others though they would not drink.

Robert Leighton: Works (on the Seventh Commandment)

There is not anything [that] will more readily dry up the sweetness and spiritual moisture of the soul, and cause the graces in it to wither, than the impure fire of lust; therefore you that have any beginnings of grace, and would have it flourish, beware of this, and quench it in its first sparkles; if you do not, it may in a little time rise above your power, and still prove very dangerous.

If you would be freed from the danger and importunity of this evil [i.e., lust], make use of these usual and very useful rules.

1. To be sober and temperate in diet; withdraw fuel.
2. Be modest and circumspect in your carriage; guard your ears and eyes, and watch over all your deportment; beware of undue and dangerous familiarities with any, upon what pretence soever.
3. Be choice in your society, for there is much in that.
4. In general, fly all occasions and incentives to uncleanness; but truly the solid care must begin within, otherwise all these outward remedies will prove but empiric medicines, as they call them.

Ezekiel Hopkins: Works (on the Fifth Commandment)

Another duty of the wife is Modesty; and that, both in Apparel and Behaviour.

1. In Apparel: that it be according to her place and rank; not affecting gaudiness or strange fashions; nor yet affecting, on the contrary, a singularity of obsoleteness and outworn antiquity; for pride may be equally shown either way. The best temper is, for them not to wear garments to be taken notice of. [He quotes 1 Peter 3:3–4 & 1 Timothy 2: 9–10.] This indeed is the best ornament; that which makes them lovely in the sight of God; and that, too, which makes them esteemed by all sober and serious persons. . . .
2. As she must be modest in her apparel, so in her Behaviour and Deportment. Here countenance, gesture, and speeches

must be all fitted to show the inward calmness and seren-
ity of her mind; and therefore, imperious, clamorous, and
turbulent women . . . are a torment and vexation to themselves, and more, to their husbands.

Martin Luther: Works (on 1 Timothy 2:9–10)

The women should be properly arranged, *correct in their apparel.*
. . . As Scripture has spoken about the purity of hands, so
women ought to walk that they may not offend someone with
their adornment. Rather, as we say in the proverb: "Decency is
women's most beautiful adornment." Simple garb and adornment is more fitting for a woman than a wagonload of pearls. .
. . He condemns those women who parade in luxury, who wish
to be dressed in the most beautiful clothing to allure lovers day
after day. . . . Paul forbids the surrendering of self to elegance,
the pompous pursuit of adornment. . . . Paul is speaking against
pomp and excess, a passion for fashion with which so many are
so affected that they cannot fill their eyes. . . .

[How does a woman dress with a good conscience?] Not for
passion or pleasure but for "apparel," that is, edifying apparel,
which offends, entraps, or scandalizes the eyes of no one.

Here (v. 10) he explains what he means by clean and deco-
rous clothing. They dress in such a way to be the sort of women
who have a zeal for piety and who practice good works. If they
overdress, it means they are self-seekers, they feed their own
eyes, they irritate others. This is to be eager for the vanity of
this world and to desire a badge for praise. Our women ought
to dress so that one can recognize that not one of them is seeking clothing. She goes about, covered everywhere. She does not
dress expensively. Whatever is left she spends on the poor. So it
appears that they are concerned about God and their neighbor
and do not seek their own praise.

John Calvin: Commentaries (on 2 Timothy 2:9–10)

He [Paul] intended to embrace the opportunity of correcting a vice to which women are almost always prone and which perhaps at Ephesus, being a city of vast wealth and extensive merchandise, especially abounded. That vice is—excessive eagerness and desire to be richly dressed. He wishes therefore that their dress should be regulated by modesty and sobriety; for luxury and immoderate expense arise from a desire to make a display either for the sake of pride or of departure from chastity. . . .

Yet we must always begin with the dispositions; for where debauchery reigns within, there will be no modesty in the outward dress. . . . It would be great baseness to deny the appropriateness of modesty as the peculiar and constant ornament of virtuous and chaste women, or the duty of all to observe moderation. Whatever is opposed to these virtues it will be vain to excuse. He expressly censures certain kinds of superfluity, such as curled hair, jewels, and golden rings; not that the use of gold or of jewels is expressly forbidden, but that, wherever they are prominently displayed, these things commonly draw along with them the other evils which I have mentioned, and arise from ambition or from want of chastity as their source.

Bibliography

Alford, Henry. *The New Testament for English Readers*, Grand Rapids: Baker, 1983.

Alsop, Vincent. *Practical Godliness: The Ornament of All Religion*. Morgan, PA: Soli Deo Gloria Publications, 2003 [1696].

Atkinson, David J., and David H. Field, eds. *New Dictionary of Christian Ethics and Pastoral Theology*. Downers Grove: InterVarsity Press, 1995.

Barger, Lilian Calles. *Eve's Revenge: Women and a Spirituality of the Body*. Grand Rapids: Brazos Press, 2003.

Barnes, Albert. *Barnes Notes*. Grand Rapids: Baker Book House, n.d.

Baumgarten, Linda. *What Clothes Reveal: The Language of Clothing in Colonial and Federal America*. Williamsburg, VA: Colonial Williamsburg Foundation and Yale University Press, 2002.

Berbrugge, Verlyn D., ed., *New International Dictionary of New Testament Theology*, abridged ed. Grand Rapids: Zondervan, 2000.

Blankenhorn, David. *Fatherless America: Confronting Our Most Urgent Social Problem*. New York: Basic Books, 1995.

Boardman, George Dana. *The Ten Commandments*. Philadelphia: American Baptist Publication Society, 1889.

Boston, Thomas. *The Complete Works of Thomas Boston*. Stoke-on-Trent: Tentmaker Publications, 2004.

Bork, Robert. *Slouching Towards Gomorrah*. New York: HarperCollins, 1996.

Brakel, Wilhelmus à. *The Christian's Reasonable Service*. Grand Rapids: Reformation Heritage Books, 1999.

Brooks, Thomas. *The Works of Thomas Brooks*. Carlisle, PA: Banner of Truth, 1980 [1861–67].

Brown, Colin, ed., *The New International Dictionary of New Testament Theology*. Grand Rapids: Zondervan, 1986.

Bruce, A. B. *The Training of the Twelve*. Edinburgh: T. & T. Clark, 1883.

Buchanan, Margaret. *Parenting with Purpose*. Grand Rapids: Baker, 2003.

Bullinger, Henry. *The Decades (First and Second)*. Cambridge: Parker Society, 1849.

Calvin, John. *Calvin's Commentaries*. Grand Rapids: Baker Book House, 1993.

Charnock, Stephen. *The Existence and Attributes of God*. Grand Rapids: Baker, 1979 rpt.

Clarke, Adam. *The Holy Bible, Containing the Old and New Testaments*. New York: Carlton & Porter, 1856.

Bibliography

Custance, Arthur. *The Doorway Papers*. Grand Rapids: Zondervan, 1975.

Dabney, Robert Lewis. *Systematic Theology*. Carlisle, PA: The Banner of Truth Trust, 2002 [1871].

———. *Discussions*. Carlisle, PA: Banner of Truth, 1982.

DeMoss, Nancy Leigh, ed. *Biblical Womanhood in the Home*. Wheaton: Crossway Books, 2002.

Douma, J. *The Ten Commandments: Manual for the Christian Life*. Nelson Kloosterman, ed. Phillipsburg, NJ: Presbyterian and Reformed Publishing, 1996 [1992].

Durham, James. *A Practical Exposition of the Ten Commandments*. Dallas: Naphtali Press, 2002 [1675].

Ethridge, Shannon, and Stehphen Arterburn. *Every Young Woman's Battle*. Colorado Springs: Waterbrook Press, 2004.

Elliot, Elisabeth. *Passion and Purity*. Grand Rapids: Fleming H. Revell, 2002.

Evans, Caroline. *Fashion at the Edge*. New Haven: Yale University Press, 2003.

Fairweather, William. *The Background of the Gospels*. Minneapolis: Klock & Klock Publishers, 1977 [1920].

Ferguson, Sinclair. *The Sermon on the Mount*. Carlisle, PA: Banner of Truth, 2002.

Grant, George. *Grand Illusions: The Legacy of Planned Parenthood*, 2nd ed. Franklin, TN: Adroit Press, 1992.

Gresh, Dannah. *And the Bride Wore White*. Chicago: Moody Press, 1999.

Guinness, Os. *The Dust of Death*. Downers Grove: InterVarsity Press, 1973.

Hall, Robert. *The Works of Robert Hall*. London: Holdsworth and Ball, 1833.

Himmelfarb, Gertrude. *On Looking into the Abyss: Untimely Thoughts on Culture and Society*. New York: Vintage Books, 1995.

Hodge, A. A. *Evangelical Theology: A Course of Popular Lectures*. Carlisle, PA: Banner of Truth, 1976 [1890].

Hughes, Barbara. *Disciplines of a Godly Woman*. Wheaton: Crossway Books, 2001.

Impson, Beth. *Called to Womanhood*. Wheaton: Crossway Books, 2001.

James, John Angell. *The Christian Father's Present*. Morgan, PA: Soli Deo Gloria Publications, 1995 [1853].

———. *Addresses to Young Men*. Morgan: PA: Soli Deo Gloria Publications, 1995 [1860].

———. *Female Piety: A Young Woman's Guide*. Morgan, PA: Soli Deo Gloria Publications, 1995 [1860].

Kempis, Thomas à. *Of the Imitation of Christ*. London: Oxford University Press, 1940 [1470].

Knight, Robert H. *The Age of Consent: The Rise of Relativism and Corruption of Popular Culture*. Dallas: Spence Publishing Company, 1998.

Koelman, Jacobus. *The Duties of Parents*. John Vriend, trans. Grand Rapids: Baker Academic, 2003.

Lasch, Christopher. *The Culture of Narcissism*. New York: W. W. Norton & Co., 1978.

Law, William. *A Serious Call to a Devout and Holy Life*. London: Methuen & Co. LTD., 1912 [1729].

Bibliography

Leighton, Robert. *The Works of Robert Leighton.* Staffordshire, UK: Tentmaker Publications, 2002 [1839].

Lenski, R. C. H. *Commentary on the New Testament.* Peabody, MA: Hendrickson Publishers, 2001.

Mahaney, Carolyn. *Feminine Appeal.* Wheaton: Crossway Books, 2003.

Makujina, John. *Measuring the Music.* Willow Street, PA: Old Paths Publications, 2002.

Newton, John. *The Works of John Newton.* Carlisle, PA: Banner of Truth, 1985 [1820].

Oden, Thomas C., ed., *Ancient Christian Commentary.* Downers Grove: InterVarsity Press, 2000.

Orr, James, ed., *International Standard Bible Encyclopedia.* Grand Rapids: Eerdmans, 1980.

Payne, Leanne. *Crisis in Masculinity.* Wheaton: Crossway Books, 1985.

Phillips, J. B. *Your God Is Too Small.* New York: Macmillan, 1953.

Pollard, Jeff. *Christian Modesty and the Public Undressing of America.* San Antonio, TX: Vision Forum, 2001.

Plumer, William. *The Law of God.* Harrisonburg, VA: Sprinkle Publications, 1996.

Roberts, Alexander, and James Donaldson, eds. *Ante-Nicene Fathers,* Vol. 4. Peabody, MA: Hendrickson Publishers, Inc., 1994 [1885].

Rushdoony, R. J. *The Institutes of Biblical Law.* n.p.: Craig Press, 1973.

Russett, Cynthia. *Darwin in America: The Intellectual Response, 1865–1912.* San Francisco: W. H. Freeman and Company, 1976.

Ryle, J. C. *The Duties of Parents.* Sand Springs, OK: Grace and Truth Books, 2002 [1888].

Sampson, Philip J. *Six Modern Myths About Christianity and Western Civilization.* Downers Grove: InterVarsity Press, 2001.

Schlafly, Phylis. *Feminist Fantasies.* Dallas: Spence Publishing, 2003.

Shalit, Wendy. *A Return to Modesty: Discovering the Lost Virtue.* New York: The Free Press, 1999.

Shedd, W. G. T. *Orthodoxy & Heterodoxy: A Miscellany.* Klock & Klock Christian Publishers, 1981 [1893].

Spence, H. D. M., and Joseph S. Exell. *The Pulpit Commentary.* Peabody, MA: Hendrickson Publisher, n.d.

Spiegel, James. *How to Be Good in a World Gone Bad.* Grand Rapids: Kregel, 2004.

Sprague, William. *Letters on Practical Subjects to a Daughter.* Harrisonburg, VA: Sprinkle Publications, 1987.

Sproul, R. C. *Life Views.* Grand Rapids: Revell Publishing, 1986.

Taylor, Jeremy. *Holy Living and Dying.* London: Bohn Standard Library, 1857 [rpt.].

Bibliography

Taylor, Thomas. *Exposition of Titus*. Minneapolis: Klock & Klock, 1980 [1619].

Tozer, A. W. *The Knowledge of the Holy*. New York: Harper & Brothers, 1961.

Ursinus, Zacharias. *The Commentary of Dr. Zacharias Ursinus on the Heidelberg Catechism, 1562*. G. W. Williard, trans., 1852. Phillipsburg, NJ: Presbyterian and Reformed, n.d.

Verbrugge, Verlyn, ed. *The New International Dictionary of New Testament Theology, Abridged ed*. Grand Rapids: Zondervan, 2000.

Watson, Thomas. *Select Works*. Pittsburgh: United Presbyterian Board of Publication, 1871.

Weaver, Richard. *Ideas Have Consequences*. Chicago: University of Chicago Press, 1948.

Webb, Heather. *Redeeming Eve*. Grand Rapids: Baker Books, 2002.

Webster, Noah. *American Dictionary of the English Language, 5th ed*. G. & C. Merriam company, 1828; reprint ed., San Francisco: Foundation for American Christian Education, 1987.

Wells, David. *God in the Wasteland: The Reality of Truth in a World of Fading Dreams*. Grand Rapids: Eerdmans, 1994.

———. *Losing Our Virtue: Why the Church Must Recover Its Moral Vision*. Grand Rapids: Eerdmans, 1998.

———. *No Place For Truth, or, Whatever Happened to Evangelical Theology?* Grand Rapids: Eerdmans, 1993.

Wesley, John. *The Works of John Wesley, 3rd ed*. Grand Rapids: Baker, 1979 [1872].

Whitehead, John. The End of Man. Westchester, IL: Crossway Books, 1986.

Wilson, Douglas. *Federal Husband*. Moscow, ID: Canon Press, 1999.

———. *Fidelity*. Moscow, ID: Canon Press, 1999.

———. *Future Men*. Moscow, ID: Canon Press, 2001.

———. *Standing on the Promises*. Moscow, ID: Canon Press, 1997.

Notes

Full bibliographic data can be found in the Bibliography.

CHAPTER 1: THE RIGHT APPROACH

1. Spiegel, *How to Be Good in a World Gone Bad*, 139.
2. Webster, *American Dictionary of the English Language*: "modesty."
3. Shalit, *A Return to Modesty*, 83.
4. Fairweather, *The Background of the Gospels*, 13–20.
5. Ibid.

CHAPTER 2: WORLDVIEW AND WARDROBE

1. Sproul, *Life Views*, 26.
2. Weaver, *Ideas Have Consequences*, 2–3.
3. Guinness, *The Dust of Death*, 22.
4. Custance, *The Doorway Papers*, vol. 6, 214.
5. Russett, *Darwin in America*, passim.
6. *Macbeth*, V. v. 17.
7. Quoted in Guinness, *The Dust of Death*, 25.
8. Ibid., 37.
9. Quoted in Custance, *The Doorway Papers*, vol. 1, 223.
10. Quoted in Wells, *No Place for Truth*, 95.
11. Himmelfarb, *On Looking into the Abyss*, 6.
12. Pitirim Sorokin quoted in Knight, *The Age of Consent*, 32.
13. Spiegel, *How to Be Good in a World Gone Bad*, 138–39.
14. Quoted in Bork, *Slouching Towards Gomorrah*, 138.
15. *U.S. News and World Report*, February 10, 1997.
16. *Pornography and Sexual Representation: A Reference Guide*: Volume 3:21.
17. Wells, *No Place for Truth*, 267–68.
18. Shedd, *Orthodoxy and Heterodoxy*, 99.
19. Shalit, *A Return to Modesty*, 23.
20. Grant, *Grand Illusions*, 111.

CHAPTER 3: THE CULTURAL CAPTIVITY OF THE CHURCH

1. Whitehead, *The End of Man*, 31.
2. Sproul, *Life Views*, 26.
3. Wells, *No Place for Truth*, 252.
4. *World Magazine*, vol. 2, #6, May 11, 1987.
5. George Barna, "Survey Shows Faith Impacts Some Behaviors but Not Others," *The Barna Update* (www.barna.org), October 22, 2002. The Barna Research Group, Ltd., Ventura, CA.
6. Ibid.
7. George Barna, "Morality Continues to Decay" *The Barna Update* (www.barna.org), November 3, 2003. The Barna Research Group, Ltd., Ventura, CA.

CHAPTER 4: A BIBLICAL VIEW OF THE BODY

1. Quoted in Orr, ed., *International Standard Bible Encyclopedia*: "body."

2. Barger, *Eve's Revenge*, 130.

3. Ibid., 19.

4. Ibid., 20.

5. Quoted in Charnock, *The Existence and Attributes of God*, Vol. I. 220.

CHAPTER 5: MODESTY AND THE LAW OF CHRIST

1. Hodge, *Evangelical Theology*, 245.

2. Thomas Scott quoted in Plumer, *The Law of God*, 506.

3 Dabney, *Systematic Theology*, 407.

4. Ferguson, *The Sermon on the Mount*, 90.

5. Shalit, *A Return to Modesty*, 73.

6. Newton, *Works*, 6:458.

7. Wesley, *Works*, 3rd ed., 11:476.

8. Shalit, *A Return to Modesty*, 97–98.

CHAPTER 6: ROBES OF RIGHTEOUSNESS

1. James, *Female Piety*, 256–57.

2. Barnes, *Barnes Notes*, on 1 Timothy 2:9.

3. Wilson, *Federal Husband*, 44.

4. Pollard, *Christian Modesty*, 52.

5. Ibid., 65.

6. See George Grant, "Abercrombie and Porn" in *Chalcedon Report*, #437, January 2002.

7. Makujina, *Measuring the Music*, 74.

8. Albert Barnes quoted in James, *Female Piety*, 259.

9. James, ibid., 263–64.

CHAPTER 7: WOMEN PROFESSING GODLINESS

1. Quoted in Shalit, *A Return to Modesty*, 246–47.

2. Ibid., 251.

3. Shalit, *A Return to Modesty*, 251.

4. Newton, *Works*, 6:458.

5. Wesley, *Works*, 11:467–68.

CHAPTER 8: THE HIDDEN PERSON OF THE HEART

1. Wesley, *Works*

2. Hall, *Works*, 1:35.

3. Shalit, *A Return to Modesty*, 67. Emphasis added.

4. Brown, *New International Dictionary*, 3:561.

5. Lenski, *Commentary*, on 1 Timothy 2:9.

6. Quoted in Shalit, *A Return to Modesty*, 232.

7. Ibid., 250.

8. Brown, *New International Dictionary*, 1:501.

9. R. C. Trench quoted in Alford, *The New Testament for English Readers*, on 1 Timothy 2:9.

10. Lenski, *Commentary*, on 1 Timothy 2:9.

11. Taylor, *Exposition of Titus*, 269.

12. Ibid., 271.

13. Spence and Exell, *The Pulpit Commentary*, Vol. XXI. on 1 Timothy 2:9.

14. Oden, *Ancient Christian Commentary*, New Testament, Vol. IX, on 1 Timothy 2:9.

15. Calvin, *Calvin's Commentaries*, on Titus 2:3.

16. George Herbert quoted in Wesley, *Works*.

CHAPTER 9: HEARTH AND HOME

1. Ryle, *The Duties of Parents*, 6.

2. Quoted in ibid.

3. Rushdoony, *The Institutes of Biblical Law*, 182.

4. Dabney, *Discussions* 3:279.

5. Hall, *Works*, 5:252.

6. Barnes, *Barnes Notes*, on Ephesians 6:4.

7. Wilson, *Federal Husband*, 35.

8. Wells, *Losing Our Virtue*, 31.

9. Wilson, *Standing on the Promises*, 68.

10. Shakespeare, *Hamlet*, II. ii.

11. Dennis F. Kinlaw, "Sacred Pedagogy," *Touchstone* magazine, June 2003.

12. Payne, *Crisis in Masculinity*, 14. See also Blankenhorn, *Fatherless America*.

13. See Genesis 27:18–40; 48:8–10.

14. Rushdoony, *The Institutes of Biblical Law*, 192.

15. Blankenhorn, *Fatherless America*, 17.

16. See Shalit, *A Return to Modesty*, passim.

17. Ibid., 7.

18. Ibid., 7–8.

Chapter 10: In the Courts of the Lord

1. Candlish in *The Revival of Religion*, 111–12.

2. Tozer, *The Knowledge of the Holy*, 6–7.

3. Wells, *No Place for Truth*, 252.

4. Phillips, *Your God Is Too Small*.

5. Spence and Exell, *The Pulpit Commentary*, 21:37.

6. Charnock, *The Existence and Attributes of God*, 1:220.

7. Pollard, *Christian Modesty*, 66.

Chapter 11: Present Your Bodies

1. Adam Clarke, *The Holy Bible*, on 1 Timothy 2:9.

2. Barnes, *Barnes Notes*, on Matthew 22:34–40.

3. Berbrugge, *New International Dictionary*, 351.

4. *St. Louis MetroVoice*, May 1996.

5. Berbrugge, *New International Dictionary*, 351.

6. Ibid.

7. Bruce, *The Training of the Twelve*, 275.

Afterword: Modesty and Men

1. Wilson, *Federal Husband*, 49.

2. Makujina, *Measuring the Music*, 91.

Printed in the USA
CPSIA information can be obtained
at www.ICGtesting.com
JSHW082159140824
68134JS00014B/329